RUGBY

RUGBY
THE PLAYER'S HANDBOOK

M. B. ROBERTS
PHOTOGRAPHS BY RONALD C. MODRA

STERLING

New York / London
www.sterlingpublishing.com

STERLING and the distinctive Sterling logo are registered trademarks
of Sterling Publishing Co., Inc.

Library of Congress Cataloging-in-Publication Data

Roberts, M. B. (Mary Beth)
  Rugby : the player's handbook / M.B. Roberts ; photographs by
Ronald C. Modra.
      p. cm.
  Includes bibliographical references and index.
  ISBN 978-1-4027-5871-3 (pb-trade pbk. : alk. paper) 1. Rugby
football. 2. Rugby football—Pictorial works. I. Modra, Ronald C. pht.
II. Title.
  GV945.R615 2010
  796.333--dc22

                                  2009039062

10   9   8   7   6   5   4   3   2   1

Published by Sterling Publishing Co., Inc.
387 Park Avenue South, New York, NY 10016
Text © 2010 by M.B. Roberts
Photos © 2010 by Ronald C. Modra
Distributed in Canada by Sterling Publishing
c/o Canadian Manda Group, 165 Dufferin Street
Toronto, Ontario, Canada M6K 3H6
Distributed in the United Kingdom by GMC Distribution Services
Castle Place, 166 High Street, Lewes, East Sussex, England BN7 1XU
Distributed in Australia by Capricorn Link (Australia) Pty. Ltd.
P.O. Box 704, Windsor, NSW 2756, Australia

Photography by Ronald C. Modra

Sterling ISBN 978-1-4027-5871-3

For information about custom editions, special sales, premium and
corporate purchases, please contact Sterling Special Sales
Department at 800-805-5489 or specialsales@sterlingpublishing.com.

Contents

FOREWORD

USA Rugby's mission is to "Inspire America to Fall in Love with Rugby," a fast-paced sport that combines the best elements of other athletic opportunities: the grace of soccer, the speed of track, and the power of football.

Bearing that in mind, it is easy to understand just why rugby is among the fastest-growing contact sports in America from the youth to the adult level. The sport continues to evolve and grow, but one overriding principle remains constant. Rugby truly is a game for all; it provides a role for people of all shapes and sizes, young and old, be it on the pitch or along the sidelines.

Like all other rugby nations, USA Rugby is not about one team; it's about the game at every level. Our membership has grown to include more than 75,000 participants from the youth through senior level, all looking to progress, to move forward and develop. Since its establishment as the sport's national governing body in 1975, USA Rugby has dedicated itself to providing added value for our members, constantly working to raise the standards of safety and athleticism through services that grow the game.

Each year, we host several National Team–level matches as well as Men's and Women's National Championship events from the high-school to senior level that draw thousands of avid rugby supporters to stadiums and sports complexes across the country to cheer on their favorite teams.

Coupled with these main events, we continually work to offer increased opportunities to develop coaches and match officials, who are integral to the quality of the game.

Now is an exciting time to be a part of USA Rugby. Our organization is in a position to raise the status of our membership with the U.S. Olympic Committee (USOC) following the announcement of rugby's abbreviated sevens format's inclusion in the upcoming 2011 Pan-American Games in Guadalajara. Looking ahead, this is another step closer to full Olympic recognition and possible inclusion in the 2016 Olympics.

In addition to opening doors on an international scale, our organization has turned its attention to the future generation of rugby in the United States. We have launched a new version of the game, Rookie Rugby, which is founded on the same principle young William Webb Ellis utilized when he invented the game in the Rugby School yard—"Just pick up the ball and run with it."

Rookie Rugby is a noncontact game that that whole family can enjoy and aims to put a rugby ball in the hands of America's youth at an earlier age through school programs and physical education environments. The fact is that kids in America like to run with the ball, they like defending and attacking, they enjoy the fact that everyone can score, and they learn quickly. The challenge is to put a ball in as many young hands as we possibly can and let them feel the thrill of running, evading, and scoring. The passing takes a little longer, and the laws can get in the way—they just want to play rugby in its most basic form.

The more I travel and the more people I meet, the more confident I become about the future of rugby in the United States. It will take time to create a regular flow of world-class players to the National Team, but if we create a strong foundation for the game across the country, this will happen more quickly than many think.

It's never too late to get involved with rugby, be it as a player, coach, referee, or simply a fan. To learn more about our great sport, visit the USA Rugby Web site at www.usarugby.org.

—Nigel Melville
CEO and President
Rugby Operations,
USA Rugby

ACKNOWLEDGMENTS

While putting this book together, we were repeatedly impressed by the passion and generosity of the rugby community. Our sincere thanks goes to the folks at USA Rugby, especially Sara John, Becky Carlson, Kathy Flores, and Nigel Melville.

Thanks to our British "team rugby," Trevor and Gill Jones, for the amazing hospitality and taxi service to youth events in England. (And for the meat pies.) Also, we greatly appreciate the efforts of the Rugby Football Union's (RFU) Mark Saltmarsh.

Thanks to our Ft. Lauderdale experts, Alex Sharland and Bill Shelley, and to the fantastic high-school players from Charlotte Catholic and their coach Brendan Keane, who demonstrated skills and drills, and Charlotte Rugby coach David Hamilton, who put it all together.

Thanks to the incredibly professional folks at Cal Rugby: Anton Malko in media relations, for permission to use photographs and arranging interviews, and coaches Jack Clark and Tom Billups, for their interviews and training tips. And thanks (again!) to Jim Thompson of the Positive Coaching Alliance for permission to quote from his terrific books.

Thanks also to Nick Stanczyk for demonstrating weight training moves and to James Cordell for supervising the session at Mariner's Hospital in Tavernier, Florida. And thanks to others we met along the way including Michael Badger, who explained the game and pointed us in the right direction.

Several websites were excellent sources of background material when researching history (www.rugbyfootballhistory.com, www.rl1908.com) and famous ruggers (http://wesclark.com/rrr/, http://rugbyfootball.com/home.html). The World Rugby Museum at Twickenham was also a fantastic resource, and our thanks to Max Dunbar for his guidance and permission to photograph artifacts. And finally, thanks to the folks at The Rugby Museum in Rugby, England, for the tour and for permission to photograph items on display there.

—M.B. Roberts
—Ron Modra

1: All about Rugby

The Oval Game in a Nutshell

What is it about rugby? In the history of sport, there has hardly been a game to excite such persistent passion among players and fans. The game began humbly in Rugby, England, during the nineteenth century, sharing its roots with soccer and, later, spawning American and Australian-rules football. Today, rugby is beloved around the world. Ruggers play on hot, sandy fields in Bahrain, on muddy pitches in northern England, and in manicured stadiums in South Africa, Argentina, and rugby-mad New Zealand. Whether it's a casual club game or a World Cup final, something happens to players who pick up that oval ball. Play it once and you may be hooked for life.

WHO, WHAT, WHERE?

THE BASICS

Although rugby may seem complicated at first to those unfamiliar with the laws, the premise is simple. Two fifteen-man teams compete for a ball, which they attempt to advance down the pitch (a.k.a. the field) by kicking it or running with it. If the ballcarrier gets in trouble, she may pass to a teammate, but only sideways or backward, not downfield toward the opposing team's goal. There are several ways to score, including a try (touching the ball down in the opponents' in-goal area or on their goal line) and a goal (made by one of several types of kicks). Not surprisingly, the team with the most points at the end of the match wins.

Making a run for it.

KEEPING SCORE

Try (5 points): The grounding of the ball by an attacking player in the opposition's in-goal area.

Conversion kick (2 points): Taken from the point where the ball was grounded during the try.

Kick at goal (3 points): Taken when the opposing team is penalized.

Dropped goal (3 points): Taken from the field. The player drops the ball on the ground and attempts to kick it through the uprights after it bounces.

THE PLAYERS

Rugby is a global game, played on five continents by both men (in more than one hundred countries) and women (in some fifty-two countries). People of all ages play rugby, from the very young to players in their thirties, forties, and beyond who just can't seem to hang up their boots. This may be surprising to some, given rugby's rough-and-tumble reputation, but there's no cause for alarm. "Rugby doesn't have to be played at full speed," says Alex Sharland, director of Fort Lauderdale's Annual International

A younger rugger.

Ruggerfest. "It can be played at five miles per hour! You've got your old boys' pace, your women's pace, high-school, and club level. Rugby can be played at all of these speeds, but at every level, the laws are the same. And according to the laws, rugby is a game for all."

Indeed, rugby may be the perfect illustration of the old saying, "It takes all kinds." In this game, there is literally a position for everyone. Big or small, fast or slow, there's a place for you on the pitch. Plus, every

member of the team plays an important role in the match. Everybody is involved. Everybody has the chance to score. Fold in the short equipment list (shoes, a ball, a few pads) and it's easy to see why rugby is welcoming so many to its ranks.

THE TRADITION

In the early 1800s, schoolboys at Rugby School and other public schools in England were playing a game best described as a mish-mash of soccer and rugby. By the late 1800s, the on-field confusion caused by inconsistent rules had resolved itself into two distinct sports—Association Football (soccer) and Rugby Football (rugby)— each with its own set of laws.

Rugby, like soccer, quickly grew in popularity around the world, especially in English-speaking countries (the exception in both cases being the United States). From the start, rugby distinguished itself as a gentleman's game. No arguing with the referee. No trash-talking. No showboating. And, perhaps most important of all, always shake your opponent's hand after the match.

Modern rugby clubs have taken this tradition a few steps further. Stories of rugby players being welcomed by fellow ruggers while visiting another city or even another country are commonplace. So are stories

Top: The pitch at Rugby School. Bottom: A game for all.

of teams socializing after the match despite having just pounded each other mercilessly on the pitch. In fact, many longtime players say this is the best part of rugby: the social scene.

Another emerging tradition, especially in clubs springing up in new rugby territory, is the diversity of the players. It's not unusual to find a club whose roster includes doctors and lawyers as well as mechanics and painters. Rugby, once considered an elitist sport, may have evolved into the great equalizer.

WHAT'S IN A GAME?

When people say "rugby," they may be referring to one of several different forms of the basic game. Mostly, they mean the versions of the sport called rugby union and rugby league, the two major worldwide entities that split from each other in 1895 over the issue of professional play. Today, these two leagues govern all the amateur and pro clubs playing their respective brands of rugby worldwide.

Currently, rugby union is played in more than one hundred countries, while rugby league is played in thirty, most notably in Australia, where it is the dominant form of the sport. Originally, the only real distinction between rugby union and rugby league was just that—amateur (union) versus professional (league). But over the years, the two factions evolved into entirely different games.

Ironically, in 1995, a full century after the initial split, rugby union lifted its ban on payment for players. The reason for the original rift is gone, but two very different games remain.

| In rugby there are no winners, only survivors.

UNION VS. LEAGUE

A few major differences—along with a host of nuances—set rugby union and rugby league apart.

Union: Fifteen players per side, tries are worth 5 points, contest possession after tackle.

League: Thirteen players per side, tries are worth 4 points, surrender possession after tackle.

Common denominators: Both games are played in 80-minute matches with the same oval-shaped ball. Both count legions of zealous fans, have their own governing bodies, and stage their own World Cups.

Besides the two major codes, "rugby" may also refer to tag or touch Rugby (a noncontact version of the sport), flag rugby (a youth game played with flags or ribbons), or even quad rugby (played by ruggers in wheelchairs). There's also rugby sevens, a shorter version of the rugby union and rugby league games, played with seven players on a side and slightly different rules. And of course there are the popular rugby spin-offs, including American (gridiron) football and Australian-rules football. But in this book, we'll focus on basic rugby, specifically the rules and particulars of rugby union.

RUGBY FOR ALL

"There is much more to rugby than the full-contact, fifteen-a-side game," says Nigel Melville, USA Rugby CEO and president of Rugby Operations. "The global game of rugby offers many versions flexible enough to suit all athletic abilities, ages, and genders. Contact or noncontact, seven-a-side to fifteens, whether you are playing, coaching, or administrating, rugby truly is a game for everyone."

Young players "tackle" with flags.

Rugby vs. Football

It's often said—especially by those who don't know the game—that rugby is just gridiron football without pads. Most rugby players get fairly worked up when they hear this statement and get busy explaining the nuances of their sport.

The main difference between the two games (besides the helmets and pads) is the flow of play. In football, there are constant stops and starts. In rugby, things keep moving whenever possible, even if a player is down. If he's not seriously injured, the teams play on. Passing is allowed in both sports, but in football you pass forward, while in rugby you pass backward. The balls are similar, but rugby balls are rounder than footballs, with less pointy ends, to prevent erratic bouncing around the field.

There are eleven players on a football team, while rugby sides comprise fifteen players. All ruggers play both offense and defense, while football players mostly specialize in one or the other.

Scoring has some of the same elements in both games. A try is very similar to a touchdown, and kicks sailing between the goalposts count for points.

Although blocking is not allowed in rugby (as it is in football), in both sports, tackling is the focus of activity. In rugby, players are tackled around the waist and legs and, once they are "down," must release the ball so play may continue. This is very different from football, where the goal is to stop the ball *and* the man by bringing him to the ground. Since every rugby player will tackle and be tackled many times during any given match, he needs to learn how to keep from getting hurt.

FOOTBALL ANYONE?

Depending where you are in the world, "football" refers to one of several related, but very different, games. There's soccer. Then there's the American sport where guys with helmets and pads block, pass, run, and sometimes kick. Then there's rugby, which some (non-rugby players) describe as a blend of the two.

The games share many similarities as well as a common history. And of course, depending on where you come from, they all share the same name.

AMERICAN FOOTBALL	RUGBY	SOCCER
Super Bowl	World Cup	World Cup
Kickoff	Kickoff, scrum, or line-out	Kickoff
Stops and starts	Play on!	Play on!
Pick a side: offense or defense	Athletes play both offense and defense	Athletes play both offense and defense
Popular in the United States	Popular in Europe, Australia, New Zealand, the Caribbean, South Africa	Popular worldwide
Field: 100 x 50 yards (91.4 x 45.7 m)	Up to 130 x 100 yards (118.9 x 91.4 m)	Typically 75 x 110 yards (68.6 x 100.6 m)
Hands	Hands	No hands, except goalie
First played in 1860s	First played in early 1800s	First played in 1697 BC
Touchdowns and field goals	Tries and goals	Goals
11 players	15 players	11 players
Pads and helmets	Limited padding and headgear	Shin guards, plus gloves for goalie
Penalty flags	Cards	Cards
Cheerleaders	Football clubs	Hooligans
Mostly male players	Some women players	Women's teams everywhere

Over 25 percent of the rugby-playing population in the United States lives in the Northeast.

PROTECT YOURSELF

Rugby is an aggressive, competitive contact sport, so when players take the field, safety is always a major concern. "The responsibility for the player's welfare is placed squarely on the coach's shoulders," says Tom Billups, strength and conditioning coach at the University of California–Berkeley. "Coaches need to assure that all athletes are physically prepared for the demands of the sport and that players have been thoroughly coached in the proper techniques required to play the game safely."

Safety should also be the primary concern of referees, who are in the position to prevent injuries by managing the game, and players, who have a responsibility to themselves and other athletes on the field to play it safe.

Note: Coaches, parents, and players have many resources available to them to learn the game of rugby and to play it safely. Be sure to check out the complete "Medical and Safety Guide" from USA Rugby and the *Rugby Ready* program from the International Rugby Board.

Safety first. Always.

Who's in Charge?

IRB

The International Rugby Board (IRB), headquartered in Dublin, Ireland, is the world governing and lawmaking body for the game of rugby union. Founded in 1886 by the unions of England, Ireland, Wales, Scotland, France, New Zealand, Australia, and South Africa, the IRB today counts ninety-six unions as full members, along with nineteen associate members and six regional associations.

Basically, the IRB's role is to promote, foster, and extend the game and to maintain and develop its laws. The IRB is constantly evaluating the laws to improve safety and the flow of the game. It does this in part by implementing Experimental Law Variations (ELVs), proposed amendments to the *Laws of the Game* that are tested on the field and sometimes added to the *Laws*. The ELVs usually result in several small changes every few years.

The IRB also provides many resources to its members, including grants, coaching instruction, and education and development programs.

Several tournaments are administered by the IRB, including the Women's Rugby World Cup, Rugby World Cup Sevens, IRB Sevens, IRB Junior World Championship, IRB Junior World Rugby Trophy, IRB Nations Cup, and the granddaddy of them all, The Rugby World Cup.

Rugby tournaments are hotly contested worldwide.

National Teams

Almost every IRB member union fields a national team or teams, all-star sides usually made up of the best players from different clubs. National teams compete against each other in the Olympics, the Rugby World Cup, and other international tournaments known as "tests," as well as occasional exhibition matches known as "friendlies." After the competition, national team players usually return to their local clubs.

The United States fields several national teams, all nicknamed the Eagles: Women's, Men's, Boys' Under-17, Men's Under-19, Women's

Under-19, Women's Under-23, All-American Team, and Sevens (both Men's and Women's).

There is a simple reason why fans get so *fanatical,* about the Rugby World Cup and other competitions featuring play between national teams: the games are country vs. country. National pride is on the line.

Major international annual championship tournaments include:

SIX NATIONS CHAMPIONSHIP: Played among England, Scotland, Wales, Ireland, France, and Italy

TRI NATIONS SERIES: Played between Australia, New Zealand, and South Africa

CHURCHILL CUP: Played between Canada, England Saxons, New Zealand Maori, Scotland A, Ireland A, and the United States.

Movie star Russell Crowe lost his front tooth playing rugby when he was ten. He didn't get it fixed until many years later when the director of "The Crossing" asked him to do so. Crowe played rugby for Sydney Boys High School and, before he became an actor, aspired to be a pro footballer. Today, he is part owner of the South Sydney Rabbitohs of the National Rugby League.

IN THEIR CUPS (AND PLATES)

Many tournaments toast the winners with a coveted prize.

Air New Zealand Cup: Formerly the National Provincial Championship (NPC); New Zealand's top domestic competition, contested by fourteen provincial unions in the first division and twelve in the second.

Bledisloe Cup: Named for Lord Bledisloe, the former governor general of New Zealand; an annual competition between Australia and New Zealand

Calcutta Cup: An annual match played between England and Scotland as part of the Six Nations

Currie Cup: South Africa's premier provincial competition, named for Sir Donald Currie, a Scotsman who originally donated the cup as a cricket trophy

EDF Energy Cup: Also known as the Anglo-Welsh Cup; the England/Wales knock-out cup, begun in 1972 as the John Player Cup; has changed names several times to reflect its major sponsor

European Cup: Also known as the Heineken Cup; a twenty-four-team tournament contested among club and provincial teams from England, France, Ireland, Italy, Scotland, and Wales

European Challenge Cup: The secondary European championship

Hopetoun Cup: Competition between Australia and Scotland

Lansdowne Cup: Competition between Australia and Ireland

Mandela Plate: Competition between Australia and South Africa

Melrose Cup: Awarded to Sevens World Cup champs

Webb Ellis Cup: The Rugby World Cup Trophy

THE RUGBY WORLD CUP

Since the first staging of the event in 1987, the Rugby World Cup has grown into a huge quadrennial extravaganza—one of the top sporting events in the world, along with the Olympics and the World Cup of soccer. According to the IRB, some 2.2 million fans attended Rugby World Cup matches in 2007 and more than 4 billion people watched the qualifying and final events on television. IRB.com recorded over 1.8 million hits during the tournament's run.

USA Rugby

In 1975, the United States of America Rugby Football Union (USARFU) was established so that American rugby would have a centralized governing body and could organize a team to compete internationally. Today, the renamed USA Rugby not only supports the efforts of several national men's and women's teams, but counts more than seventy-five thousand members playing youth, high-school, collegiate, and post-collegiate rugby.

USA Rugby offers many valuable services to its members, from educational training for refs and coaches to liability insurance for clubs. The national office, located in Boulder, Colorado, oversees seven territorial unions and thirty-seven local area unions and hosts annual national championships for men and women at all levels. (Check out http://www.usarugby.org to learn more.)

Youth

In many parts of the world, kids grow up playing rugby. Not so in the United States, where the average age of first-time players is nineteen. USA Rugby is hoping to change that by making a push to get more young players onto the rugby pitch. "The key to growing men's and women's rugby in this country is getting the ball into the hands of kids," says USA Rugby's Becky Carlson.

The first line of attack? The Rookie Rugby program, a noncontact youth initiative targeted at players age six to twelve. The second? USA Rugby's partnership with Play Rugby USA, a national youth development program that teaches flag rugby (a noncontact version of the sport) to kids.

Noncontact rugby, whether it's touch or flag, is the ideal version of the sport for boys and girls age ten and under. In touch rugby, the ballcarrier is stopped with a two-handed touch or tag. In flag rugby, the ballcarrier is stopped when a flag is removed from her belt. Since there is no tackling allowed during these games, players focus on moving the ball up and down the field (and parents don't have to worry about their kids getting hurt). As in the grown-up version of the sport, every player gets the chance to handle the ball and to play both offense and defense.

Start 'em young.

The goal is to give a young player experience so that when he turns eleven, he can move on to a youth club that plays contact rugby and start to add tackling to his skills.

USA Rugby offers support to youth coaches and referees through Rookie Rugby and its Youth Development Network weekly e-newsletter. Another feather in its cap is the Youth & High School Strategic Plan, which outlines a strategy of identifying local youth leaders to promote the sport and assist with developing programs.

High School

The greatest growth within USA Rugby now is taking place in the under-eighteen age group. From 1999 to 2007, the number of high-school clubs in the United States more than doubled—from 226 to 555. As positive as this trend may be, the fact remains that only a handful of high-school rugby clubs are actually sponsored by schools.

What this means is that high-school rugby is not an officially recognized National Federation of State High School Associations (NFHS) sport, such as soccer or football. The term "high-school team" refers to a club made up of high-school age players from the same school or from several schools in the same area. The bottom line for club sports versus school-sponsored sports is resources. Nonsanctioned clubs must recruit their own coaches and pay for their own uniforms, transportation, and so on.

The good news? Rugby is expected to be the next emerging sport recognized by the NFHS.

Even though rugby is still digging in at the high-school level, USA Rugby has been crowning a national high-school boys' champion every year since 1985 at the National High School Championship Tournament.

According to the Sporting Goods Manufacturers Association, there were 316,000 people playing rugby in the United States in 2007.

University of California repeat champs. *Photo credit: Cal Media Relations, Kelley Cox, Michael Pimentel.*

"Playing rugby at school, I once fell on a loose ball and, through ignorance and fear, held on despite a fierce pummeling. After that, it took me months to convince my teammates I was a coward." —COMEDIAN PETER COOK

(Highland Rugby Club of Salt Lake City, Utah, featured in the 2008 movie *Forever Strong,* has taken the top prize seventeen times!)

As rugby grows in popularity in the United States, fans will be seeing more American high-school teams (such as Highland, which competed in 1998) at competitions such as the World Schools Rugby Championship.

College

Most of the nearly thirty thousand college rugby players are playing the sport for the first time. Often, these players are high school athletes who excelled at other sports, especially football, but didn't have the size, ability, or desire to make those college teams. For them, rugby offers an excellent opportunity to play a challenging and rewarding sport.

At some schools, such as the University of California–Berkeley, rugby is more than just an up-and-coming sport. Of Cal's twenty-seven varsity sports, rugby is the most successful. The team, which has won the National Collegiate Rugby Championships an incredible twenty-four out of twenty-nine times since 1980, has been on campus since 1882, longer than any other sport except for crew. Since rugby is not NCAA-sanctioned, Cal Rugby can't award scholarships to its players. Nonetheless, the team has top-rate facilities on campus and remains financially self-sufficient thanks to enthusiastic alumni and donor support.

Some college clubs, such as Texas A&M, New Mexico University, Penn State, and Palmer Chiropractic, do offer scholarships from alumni endowments, sponsor grants, or other sources. College-bound athletes interested in rugby will definitely want to research these opportunities. (Contact USA Rugby for up-to-date information.)

You Go, Girl!

Girls play rugby? Every woman playing rugby today has heard that question. The answer is a resounding *yes*. Women and men play by the same rules at every level of the game. (Note: In countries where rugby is popular, such as England, very young boys and girls often play on teams together.) The number one reason women give for playing rugby is the contact: There is no other full-contact sport for women on the planet. Once women play rugby, they get addicted to the game the same way the guys do.

High-School Women

As of 2007, there were more than 150 high-school clubs playing girls' rugby in the United States. If this number sounds somewhat small, look at it from a more impressive angle: Women's rugby at the high-school level grew nearly 10,000 percent between 2002, when there were fifty players enrolled, and 2008, when there were five thousand.

At first, none of the clubs were sanctioned by their schools. But then, in the fall of 2008, Sebastian River High School in Sebastian, Florida, broke the mold and became the first school to officially sponsor girls' varsity rugby. (All eyes are on Colorado schools to add programs soon.)

More and more girls are getting into the game.

Just as for male players, the main concern for female players of youth and high-school rugby, and for their parents, is safety. In both the girls' and the boys' game, the responsibility lies with the refs (to enforce the laws) and the coaches (to teach safe and proper technique). For this reason, USA Rugby is pushing hard for more high schools to officially adopt varsity rugby. "When a team has a full-time coach, and players get supervision and guidance on weight training and diet, this cuts down injuries by 75 percent," says Becky Carlson, USA Rugby's Emerging Sports Program Manager. "This holds true for any sport. Give them guidance and resources and you're going to see fewer injuries."

Parents will be glad to know that studies by the Committee on Competitive Safeguards and Medical Aspects of Sports (CSMAS) have shown that the injury rates in women's rugby are no higher than those in women's soccer. There's no reason that female players can't safely play the game that USA Rugby describes as "a running game which combines the grace of soccer, the power of football and the speed of track."

"The game is more than just contact," says Carlson. "You have some great long runs. You have some great defense. If players are coached right, conditioned well and don't have too many games in their schedule, rugby can be played safely."

COLLEGE WOMEN

Like their male counterparts, the majority of American women players kick off their rugby careers in college. (Incredibly, though, many female players—in the United States and around the world—don't pick up the game until after graduation. Sharon Whitehead, who plays the position of loosehead prop for England, first took up rugby in her twenties and didn't make her debut on the women's national team until she was thirty-one! No doubt this trend will slow as more and more women get involved in rugby at the high-school level.)

In 2002, Division I Women's Rugby was classified as a National Collegiate Athletic Association (NCAA) emerging sport. In 2004, Divisions II and III were added to the classification. In 2008, there were some 350 women's collegiate rugby clubs. Of these, five are NCAA-sanctioned programs. If and when women's rugby is officially and fully taken under the wing of the NCAA, the support for the game on campus will explode.

SCRUMS OF HIGHER LEARNING

Many coaches, fans, and players in the know say that college rugby teams are the best ambassadors for the sport in the United States. Perennial college powerhouses include twenty-four-time national champion University of California-Berkeley, along with always-competitive Air Force, Army, Navy, Harvard, Penn State, San Diego State, BYU, Colorado, Dartmouth, Stanford, Wyoming, and Miami (Ohio). Others to watch out for are Maryland, Long Beach State, Utah, Ohio State, Illinois, Kansas State, Life College, and Radford (2008 Division II champions), just to name a few.

FROM SCRUMHALF TO WHO'S WHO

Does playing rugby guarantee success in later life? Maybe not. But here's a powerfully persuasive list of former players with boldface names.

Past and Present NFL Players:

Gary Anderson
Shawn Bradley
Randy Cross
Dave Dalby
David Dixon
Jim Gibbons
Haloti Ngata
John Sciarra
Fran Tarkenton
Steve Tasker

Other Sporting Types:

John Amaechi (NBA)
Mark Cuban (NBA Dallas
   Mavericks owner)
Ernie Els (golfer)
Ryan Giggs (Manchester
   United soccer star)
Andre the Giant (wrestler)
Owen Hart (wrestler)
Eric Liddell (runner and
   Olympic gold medalist)
James Naismith (inventor of
   basketball)
Jacques Rogge
   (International Olympic
   Committee President)

Stars of Stage and Screen:

Richard Burton
Charlie Chaplin
Sean Connery
Peter Cook
Daniel Crai
Russell Crowe
Chris Farley
Mark Harmon
Richard Harris
Boris Karloff
Meat Loaf
David Niven
Peter O'Toole

Princes and Politicos:

Che Guevara
Ted Kennedy
Prince William
Prince Harry

Prime ministers:

Gordon Brown (U.K.)
Winston Churchill (U.K.)
Yoshio Mori (Japan)

Presidents:

George W. Bush (U.S)
Jacques Chirac (France)
Bill Clinton (U.S)
John F. Kennedy (U.S)
Roh Tae-woo (South Korea)

Dictators:

Idi Amin (Uganda)
Benito Mussolini (Italy)

Authors:

Raymond Chandler
Sir Arthur Conan Doyle
James Herriot
James Joyce
J.R.R. Tolkien
P.G. Wodehouse

And . . .

Andy Capp (comic strip
   character)
Brian Epstein (Beatles
   manager)
Bill Ford, Jr. (Ford CEO)
Sir Edmund Hillary (explorer)
Trevor Rees-Jones
   (former Princess Diana
   bodyguard)
Robert Mondavi
   (winemaker)
Tony O'Reilly (chairman of
   Heinz Foods)

SIR! YES SIR!

Teams from the military schools are consistently competitive in rugby. Since the beginning of the collegiate national championships in 1980, Air Force has taken the top prize three times, finished second five times, and finished third four times. Army and Navy are always in the mix, counting a dozen second-, third-, and fourth-place finishes between them.

Why is this?

Some say that these athletes, who are used to boot camp and basic training, actually enjoy rugby. To them, it's a day off.

THE BIG TIME

THE PROS

Ever since rugby union began permitting play for pay in 1995, both rugby codes, union and league, are played at both the amateur and the professional level throughout the world. All the leading rugby nations sponsor their own professional leagues, such as National Rugby League (featuring rugby league teams) in Australia or the Courage League (featuring rugby union teams) in England. Most countries further segment their leagues into provincial divisions whose teams play each other, then send champions to compete against other divisions in inter-provincial play. Fans of professional rugby don't have to look hard to find matches being played just about any time of year. Whether it's the London Wasps in the Guinness Premiership or the Celtic Crusaders in the Super League, rugby rarely rests.

> "Rugby is a wonderful show: dance, opera, and suddenly, the blood of a killing."
>
> —ACTOR AND EX-FLANKER RICHARD BURTON

Big Crowds...

- 109,874 fans watched New Zealand's 39–35 win over Australia at Stadium Australia, Sydney, Australia, on July 15, 2000.

- A three-day sellout crowd of 120,000 fans attended the IRB Rugby World Cup Sevens 2005 tournament in Hong Kong.

- More than 50,000 fans packed Melbourne's Telstra Dome for the Rugby Sevens final during the 2006 Commonwealth Games.

...And Big Stadiums

- Croke Park, Dublin, Ireland, 82,000

- Eden Park, Auckland, New Zealand, 45,472

- Ellis Park, Johannesburg, South Africa, 60,000

- Millennium Stadium, Cardiff, Wales, 76,250

- Telstra Stadium, Sydney, Australia, 83,500

- Twickenham, London, England, 82,000

- Stade de Paris, Paris, France, 80,000

Talk about a "Hail Mary": Larrivire-St. Savin, a town located 150 kilometers south of Bordeaux, France, boasts the only church in the world dedicated to rugby union. Notre-Dame-du-Rugby was dedicated in 1963 by Father Michel Devert after three players from the local club died in a car accident. To this day, dozens of donated jerseys decorate the sanctuary, along with a stained glass window depicting scrums, line-outs, and other plays.

TOP-LEVEL RUGBY IN THE UNITED STATES

Top-tier club players in the United States compete in the Super League (not to be confused with the European organization of the same name), which was launched in 1997 and sanctioned by USA Rugby in 2001 as the highest level of competition in the United States.

Although a few players (usually European recruits) receive some compensation, the teams are not considered professional since most players are not paid, at least not enough to earn a living. Rugby players in the United States have day jobs and play for the love of the game.

Top American players shoot for the Super League.

The Super League, which plays a spring schedule (March–May), is divided into two conferences, Red and Blue, comprising eight teams each. Super League teams play according to the rugby union code. Top-tier rugby league players in the United States play in the American National Rugby League (AMNRL), established in 1998 with ten teams competing.

RUGBY SUPER LEAGUE TEAMS

Red Conference:
Belmont Shore, Chicago Griffins, Chicago Lions, Denver, Old Mission Beach, Old Puget Sound Beach, San Francisco Golden Gate, and Santa Monica

Blue Conference:
Boston, Boston Irish Wolfhounds, Charlotte, Dallas, Life University, New York Athletic Club, New York Old Blue, and Potomac

(http://usarugbysuperleague.com)

AMERICAN NATIONAL RUGBY LEAGUE TEAMS

- Aston DSC Bulls
- Bucks County Sharks
- Connecticut Wildcats
- Fairfax Eagles

- Jacksonville Axemen
- New Haven Warriors
- New York Knights
- Northern Raiders

- Philadelphia Fight
- Washington D.C. Slayers

(http://www.amnrl.com)

"I prefer rugby over (American) football because football stops and starts so much. In rugby, they go hell for leather, nonstop. That's why if you get knocked down, you don't lay there unless you're really injured."—GAVIN, IRISH BARTENDER, KAVANAUGH & MORRISSEYS, PLANTATION, FLORIDA

Nothing quite like watching it in person.

RUGBY ON THE TUBE

Even though some 238 channels across the globe broadcast the 2007 World Cup, it wasn't long ago that rugby fans in the United States were hard-pressed to find their game on TV. Quick blips could be seen on ABC's Wide World of Sports in the 1970s or on ESPN in the 1980s, but mostly, hard-core followers were forced to seek out satellite broadcasts at their favorite English pubs, often in the middle of the night. Then, with the explosion of cable and satellite TV, things began to change.

In 1995, Championship Rugby, a weekly program, came on the air, running through 2003. The Rugby Club followed in 2004 but was canceled when its network, Fox Sports World, morphed into the all-soccer Fox Soccer Channel.

Today, there are several options for rugby viewing in the United States. Check out Versus, a basic cable station, or Setanta Sports, a network available in North America from several different pay providers such as DIRECTV and DISH Networks.

For more information on where to find rugby on TV, check the Internet (try http://www.rugbyontv.com). Or, if you're game, watch matches directly on Internet feeds at http://www.rugbyzone.com (formerly http://www.mediazone.com), which carries some 250 live and downloadable matches per year.

Watch This!

- Some 300 million TV viewers tuned in for the first Rugby World Cup in 1987.

- The 2005–06 IRB Sevens World Series was televised by thirty-two international broadcasters in eleven different languages with a potential cumulative audience reach of more than 475 million.

Sevens Up!

Rugby sevens (mostly referred to by players and fans as "sevens"), is rugby's quicker, shorter, higher-scoring little brother. Played on the same size field as regular rugby, sevens is an abbreviated form of the game in which teams of seven players (as opposed to fifteen) compete for 15 minutes per half (as opposed to 40). Competition finals run 20 minutes per half.

The upside of this format, where many stars of the fifteen-player game have emerged, is that entire tournaments can be played in a weekend or even a day. (This has been a big selling point in the IRB's push to reinstate rugby in the Olympics, where it has not been played since 1924.) Sevens has been a boon to the national teams of smaller countries, whose player pools are not as deep as those of rugby stalwarts. And sevens is an excellent game for youth players, since with fewer players on the field everyone gets more opportunities to handle the ball.

Players need to be fast and fit to play sevens, since fewer players cover the same amount of field and have less time to score. The rules are similar, with a few significant differences:

- Scrums are composed of just three players per team.
- Conversion attempts must be drop kicks and must be attempted within 40 seconds after a try is scored.
- Suspended players are "sin-binned"—put in the penalty box—for only 2 minutes (as opposed to 10 in the regular game).
- After a score, the scoring team kicks to the opposition from a spot in the center of the field.

Courtesy of the World Rugby Museum.

2: THE STORY OF RUGBY

From Legends and Laws to Playing for Pay

When does a game that scores of people play in different ways on opposite sides of the world officially become a sport? Most people go by the day the rules are agreed upon and written. But what fun is that? A sport as thrilling and colorful as rugby needs a story. Something to bolster its rebellious reputation.

William Webb Ellis was first referred to as the father of rugby in a Rugby School magazine in 1875, four years after his death. The article was written by Matthew Bloxham, an old Rugbean who sought to disprove the idea that rugby was an ancient game.

Years after he "picked up the ball," William Webb Ellis became the rector of St. Clement Dane church from 1843–1855.

Rugby Roots

A Fine Disregard for the Rules

As the legend goes, in 1823, a student at Rugby School in England—young William Webb Ellis—picked up the ball and ran with it during a football (soccer) game. At the time, even though the game was still evolving and there were no official rules, this just wasn't done.

Was Webb Ellis the first football player to handle the ball with his hands? Definitely not. Did he invent rugby? Not likely. In fact, he was not credited with this great feat, which is commemorated on a monument in Rugby, England, until several years after his death.

Commemorating the first pick-up.

Several historical facts are beyond dispute. William Webb Ellis was indeed a pupil and a sportsman at Rugby School in 1823 and, like most of his classmates, played a version of "football" that looked more like rugby than soccer. Webb Ellis went on to attend Oxford University, where, interestingly, he played in the school's first cricket match against Cambridge. He later became a cler-

A plaque honors William Webb Ellis on the school grounds in Rugby, England.

gyman and died in Menton, France, in 1872. To this day, rugby players make pilgrimages to his grave and, more fittingly, to Rugby, where the game spent its formative years.

HOOLIGANS THROUGH HISTORY

Although modern rugby traces its roots directly to nineteenth-century England, historians note that people have been playing games that displayed elements of rugby for centuries. For the ancient Romans, it was harpastum, a game played with a small ball on a rectangular field; though it is often called an early form of soccer, it resembled rugby more, since teams fought for possession of the ball and often carried it with their hands. Medieval Irishmen played cad, in which they carried a ball (usually an inflated pig's bladder) into a goal (typically two trees bent toward each other and tied together to form an arch). Centuries ago, Welshmen played cnappan, a game played on religious feast days in which teams, often comprising dozens or even hundreds of players, fought for possession of a wooden ball. The French played soule and Eastern Europeans played lelo. And as early as the third century AD, Englishmen burst into spontaneous games of mob football, a mish-mash of soccer, rugby, and all-out war that often involved entire villages and sometimes resulted in property damage, injury, and even death.

This mob version of the game, with few rules and plenty of violence, was played for centuries in England and surrounding countries, except during periods when it was outlawed by local or national authorities. According to *A Game for Hooligans: The History of Rugby Union*, early versions of football were declared illegal in England, Scotland, and Wales on thirty-one different occasions between 1314 and 1667.

By the Rules

From the Street to the Schoolyard

Football wasn't always unlawful and violent, but until the early 1800s it remained a "mob" game, meaning that teams didn't consist of a set number of players, but played with whatever cluster of people happened to show up that day. Rules were loose, when they were followed at all. Not surprisingly, football was mostly frowned upon by the upper classes, although some authorities grudgingly admitted that the sport constituted a useful distraction from less desirable occupations, such as heavy drinking and gambling.

Before bubblegum: Early on, players collected and traded team cards. *Courtesy of the World Rugby Museum.*

Things changed dramatically when Britain's prestigious public schools began to embrace organized sport in the mid-1800s. Soon football was not only allowed, it was a compulsory part of the curriculum at many schools.

In the 1840s, "football" was still a broad term, and there was confusion when schools and clubs played each other, because rules (usually passed along by word of mouth) varied from place to place. At first, each school made its own rules depending on factors such as the particular playing space available. For example, schools such as Charterhouse, Westminster, and Eton played on smaller playgrounds, some of them paved and surrounded by brick walls. Obviously, this limited the number of players who could occupy the field and the type of contact they could make with one another, so it makes sense that players mostly kicked the ball, as opposed to running with it and tackling each other.

Schools such as Cheltenham and Rugby, on the other hand, played on expansive outdoor fields, where players had room to run. Since there were no brick walls to slam into, it's not surprising that a more rough-and-tumble version of the sport developed here.

Sometimes, the rules varied a lot. According to *A Game for Hooligans*, in 1839, players in Cambridge were wary of reports they'd heard of Rugby men "playing a new game in which they made a circle around a ball and butted each other." Team captains dealt with the variation as best they could by meeting before matches to agree on standards for play.

The Rugby version of the game took off across England. *Courtesy of the World Rugby Museum.*

In 1845, Rugby School became one of the first to commit football rules to paper. In fact, since their rules included provisions for running with the ball, it's fair to say that they were the first to codify the version of the game that would become rugby. Then, in 1848, representatives from all the major British public schools, including Rugby, met in Cambridge with the goal of standardizing the rules of the game. The contentious seven-hour summit that produced the Cambridge Rules culminated in a vote on ball handling (the major issue) that limited players to catching the ball and immediately kicking it away.

For the next decade or so, football continued to evolve, with each school still playing mostly by its own rules or even switching between different codes, depending on the opponent. Former schoolboy players who wanted to continue to play formed collegiate teams or town clubs such as Guy's Hospital in London, Liverpool RFU, and Blackheath Club, often recruiting new players to join them. During this time, the proto-rugby version of football was also taking hold outside England by way of school teams and local clubs in Ireland, Scotland, Wales, Germany, South Africa, and Australia.

THE SPLIT

Despite attempts to find common ground, footballers continued to strongly disagree on fundamental points of the game. So, on October 26, 1863, eleven English teams sent representatives to the Freemason's Tavern in London to set down rules for the Football Association (FA) once and for all. At the end of another raucous meeting, in which the parties debated everything from hacking (shin-kicking) to pushing and tripping, the rules were set and the game to be known thenceforth as "football" (in other words, soccer) was officially born.

But several schools and clubs, including Blackheath, the most vocal of the group, would not accept the provision to forbid running with the ball and decided to break off on their own. These schools and clubs continued to play what they now began calling "Rugby football," and in 1871 they convened at the Pall Mall Restaurant in London to form their own association, the Rugby Football Union (RFU), and write their own rules. Three former Rugby pupils were charged with the task of committing the rules to

A toast to the Laws of the Game. *Courtesy of the World Rugby Museum.*

When the *Laws of the Game* was drafted in 1871, the bulk of the writing fell to L. J. Maton, who was housebound with a broken leg. He was rewarded by his fellow committee members with a supply of tobacco.

A scrum's-eye view of the evolving game, cartoon circa 1907. *Courtesy of the World Rugby Museum.*

paper. All three men were lawyers, which explains why today's rugby players abide by the Laws (as opposed to the rules) of the Game.

To Pay or Not to Pay

During its early years, when it was played mostly by young men attending England's prestigious public schools, rugby was perceived as an elitist sport. Many of the game's pioneers believed rugby should remain a purely amateur pursuit. But as more and more middle-class and working men took up the game, the question of whether players should be paid developed into a heated debate.

At first, the discussion involved the issue of "broken time": Some players wanted to be compensated when they had to miss work to play in games. Of course this didn't apply to gentlemen of means who didn't work for a living. Hence, the great divide.

After years of arguments between clubs located in predominantly working-class communities (northern England) and those in elite enclaves (the London area), the issue finally came to a head. In August of 1895, twenty-two northern clubs favoring "professionalism" seceded from the RFU and formed the Northern Rugby Football Union, which would eventually become the Rugby Football League.

To this day, rugby union and rugby league are separate entities. Initially, the only real difference was that one was professional (league) and the other was amateur (union). Over the years, the two codes evolved into two distinct games with several important differences in their rules. Ironically, in 1995, exactly one hundred years after the split, rugby union too turned professional, eliminating the disparity that originally drove the rival factions apart.

RUGBY AROUND THE WORLD

THE SPREAD

Soon, the gospel of rugby spread far and wide, mostly courtesy of British sailors, soldiers, students, and colonists, who brought the game with them when they visited or emigrated to different parts of the world. By the early 1900s, rugby was being played in most of Europe as well as South Africa, the United States, Canada, Australia, and New Zealand, where it was becoming wildly popular.

Not surprisingly, the same argument that had divided rugby union and rugby league in England consumed other clubs around the world. In Australia, eight clubs in Sydney that were in favor of playing for pay broke away from the union and formed the New South Wales Rugby League in 1908.

With the growth of the sport came the opportunity for teams from different countries to play each other. The first international match

Wales puts its opponent on notice. *Courtesy of the World Rugby Museum.*

England vs. Scotland became a highly anticipated match-up. *Courtesy of the World Rugby Museum.*

was played on March 27, 1871, at Raeburn Place, Edinburgh, between England and Scotland. (The Scottish team won.)

Then, in 1886, Scotland, Ireland, and Wales formed the International Rugby Football Board (IRFB), with the goal of standardizing the game for international play. England initially refused to join after the board refused its request for greater representation

Hats off! Rugby goes global. *Courtesy of the World Rugby Museum.*

based on its larger number of clubs. But in 1890, England did come on board, so to speak, and the IRFB officially became rugby's world governing and law-making body. (The board changed its name in 1997 to the International Rugby Board, or IRB.)

THE KICKOFF OF NORTH AMERICAN RUGBY

Not long after the *Laws of the Game* was written in England, the first match of record in America was played when Harvard University hosted Montreal's McGill University in Cambridge, Massachusetts. The game, in

Almost one-third of the 389 Irish rugby players who were capped [played for their national team] prior to 1914 were medics.

"What's a Rugby?"

The first recorded rugby match in the United States was between Harvard and Montreal's McGill University in 1874. The two teams agreed to play three games, one under Harvard's rules (which were basically soccer) and two under McGill's rules, which more resembled today's rugby. After the first game, which Harvard won handily playing under familiar rules, McGill's players warned, "Just wait until tomorrow when we play rugby!" The Harvard team laughed, but when the McGill players were out of earshot they asked each other nervously, "What's a rugby?"

May 1874, was the first of three proposed by McGill, two to be played in Cambridge and the third to be played in Montreal. The series presented a challenge to both sides, since (sound familiar?) each school played by different rules. The teams agreed to play one game by Harvard's rules and two by McGill's rules. This was agreeable to the Harvard players—so much so that they decided to play ever after by McGill's rules, which closely resembled the rugby being playing across the Big Pond.

Around the same time, rugby was also being played on the West Coast, primarily in the San Francisco area, where schools such as the University of California and Stanford became rugby hotbeds. Back on the East Coast, Harvard, Yale, Princeton, and Columbia formed the Intercollegiate Football Association in 1876 and played a version of football that adhered to the rugby code, except for a slight difference in scoring.

According to *Rugby for Dummies*, for the next thirty years, rugby was the primary form of "football" competition in the United States, although the game as it was played then would hardly be recognizable to today's rugby fans. This turn-of-the-century brand of rugby—and, by extension, the early form of gridiron American football—tended to be extremely violent. Following many incidents involving serious

injuries and a number of deaths, even the President got involved. Teddy Roosevelt waved his proverbial big stick to initiate reforms in the sport.

Gearing up in the early days. *Courtesy of the World Rugby Museum.*

Early in the twentieth century, as everyone knows, the gridiron version of the game took hold and took over in the United States. Except for a few rugby diehards, mostly teams from California and the Northeast, and American teams that won gold at the 1920 and 1924 Olympics, rugby all but disappeared from the United States (as well as Canada) until the 1960s.

"Rugby was brutal and raw in the late nineteenth century with 71 deaths recorded in English rugby from 1890 to 1893 alone."—RL1908.COM

THE OLYMPICS

Rugby has been played in the modern Olympic games four times: in 1900, 1908, 1920, and 1924.

At the Paris games in 1900, only three countries, Great Britain, Germany, and France, sent teams. (France won the gold.) At the London games in 1908, rugby was again represented by only three teams, Australasia (players from Australia and New Zealand), France, and Great Britain. (Australasia took the gold.) At the 1920 Antwerp games, just two teams, the United States and France, competed after Czechoslovakia and Romania withdrew. The underdog American team, made up of college players from several California schools, won the gold.

Back in Paris in 1924, the Americans again defeated France for the gold, much to the dismay of the unruly home crowd. Through no fault of said crowd, this was the last time rugby was played as an Olympic sport.

Rugby in the early twentieth century. *Courtesy of the World Rugby Museum.*

How is it that rugby, a global sport played in more than one hundred countries, is not part of the Olympic Games? Part of the explanation lies in IRB regulations, which require players of the fifteen-man game to rest seven days between matches, a nearly impossible accommodation to make within the current Olympic schedule.

Some say the solution is to promote rugby sevens as an Olympic sport. We'll come back to this in a minute.

Captains of Ireland vs. England, 1926. *Courtesy of the World Rugby Museum.*

THE WORLD CUP

For decades, national teams have been competing in exciting international tournaments such as the Six Nations Championship and the Tri Nations Series. But in 1987, rugby officially went global with the staging of the first Rugby World Cup.

Several factors fueled the campaign to organize this event, which is now held every four years. At the forefront was the desire of several countries, notably those in the Southern Hemisphere, to increase the game's worldwide visibility. Then there was the opportunity to crown a real world champion: Before the World Cup, the best team in the world was determined only through rankings and polls.

The first Rugby World Cup was a sixteen-team invitational tournament played in Australia and New Zealand, with the New Zealand All-Blacks beating the French Tricolors 29–9 in the final at Auckland's Eden Park.

In 1991, the second Rugby World Cup was played in Great Britain, Ireland, and France. Once again, sixteen teams competed, but this time, eight teams (the quarterfinalists from the 1987 World Cup) automatically qualified while the remaining eight were selected through a regional qualifying process. Australia beat England in the final (12–6) to take home the William Webb Ellis Cup, the championship trophy that many rugby players and fans affectionately call "Bill."

The 1995 World Cup was contested in South Africa, with the hosting Springboks beating the All-Blacks 15–12 in extra time during the thrilling final. In 1999, Britain, France, Ireland, and Wales shared hosting duties (with Wales as lead host) for a lineup of twenty teams. Australia defeated France 35–12 to win the championship. The next time out, in 2003, host nation Australia saw her team lose to England 20–17 in the final.

The 2007 World Cup was played in France, Wales, and Scotland, between twenty teams. South Africa beat England (15–6) to reclaim Bill. In 2011, the World Cup will be played in New Zealand.

THE U.S. MEN'S NATIONAL TEAM

USA Rugby fielded its first men's national team, the Eagles, in 1976, and played its first test match on January 31 of that year in Anaheim, California, against Australia. Although the Eagles lost the match to the formidable Wallabies (24–12), they played well, and over the years they garnered a reputation for their aggressive tackling, inspired by

American football. The Eagles ranked twentieth in the world by the IRB in 2008, won 47 out of their 149 international test matches from 1976 to 2007, and competed in several prestigious international tournaments, including the Churchill Cup and the Pan American Championship. The Eagles have also qualified for five out of the six World Cups held, missing out only in 1995.

The Eagles' most successful era was between 2006 and 2007, when they were ranked fourteenth in the world. Although the team has yet to beat world rugby powerhouses such as England, Ireland, Australia, and New Zealand, there are signs of progress as the game continues to grow in popularity in the United States and the Eagles take advantage of more opportunities to compete.

Sevens has its roots in Scotland. *Courtesy of the World Rugby Museum.*

SEVENS

Although sevens tournaments are a relatively new phenomenon in international sports, the game actually dates back to 1883, when a butcher in Melrose, Scotland, suggested staging a rugby tournament as part of his town's sports day. Fielding teams of twenty a side (the sanctioned number of players back then) was not feasible, so the butcher, David Sanderson, and his apprentice, Ned Haig, suggested reducing the number of players to seven. The tournament, in which the smaller teams played shorter matches, was a smash.

Over a century later, rugby sevens is enjoying a resurgence. In 1993, the inaugural Rugby World Cup Sevens was contested in Edinburgh,

Scotland, with England besting Australia (21–17) in the final. In 1997, the event players met in Hong Kong, with Fiji taking home the championship Melrose Cup. In 2001, the World Cup Sevens moved to Mar Del Plata, Argentina, where New Zealand won the final over Australia, 31–12. In 2005, the cup returned to Hong Kong, where Fiji won again.

Sevens competition may be the area where the U.S. Men's National Team shows the most promise. The Eagles have an excellent track record at the Hong Kong Sevens, where they won the Bowl Final in 1997 and went 3–2 in 2007. In 2003, the United States was named to host a leg of the IRB Sevens World Series, the first time an IRB-sanctioned match was played in America. The United States has hosted every year since at PETCO Park in San Diego, even winning the Shield Trophy in 2004 and 2007.

Sevens may also be rugby's ticket back to the Olympics. This version of the game does not carry the same constraints (such as number of players and required rest days) that make the fifteens format unworkable for Olympic competition. Proponents also point out that a rugby sevens tournament could be accommodated in one stadium, making it relatively inexpensive to stage.

In 1887, Jack MacCaulay became the first married man to be capped [to play for his national team] in international rugby. According to Rugby folklore, he married just to get a leave of absence from work to play for Ireland. *—ODD SHAPED BALLS: MISCHIEF MAKERS, MISCREANTS AND MAD-HATTERS OF RUGBY*

Olympic organizers cannot ignore the success and enormous attendance figures from the Sevens World Series and the World Cup Sevens tournaments. Although rugby was passed over for inclusion in the 2012 games, the sport, which has been featured in the Commonwealth Games since 1998, is a strong contender to be included in the 2016 Summer Games.

HERE COME THE GIRLS

Although it wasn't officially sanctioned by the IRB until 1998, the first Women's Rugby World Cup was played in 1991 in Wales, with twelve teams competing. The United States beat England in the final, 19–6.

Internationally, women's rugby has evolved in much the same way women's soccer has. Since women's teams are a relatively new phenomenon around the world, even in countries with long rugby traditions, newcomers to the sport have been able to compete without having to play catch-up, as men's teams in the United States, Canada, and parts of South America have had to do.

As one of the first women's teams to compete internationally, the U.S. women have been incredibly successful in international play, finishing second to England in the 1994 World Cup and second to New Zealand in the 1998 World Cup. New Zealand, whose team enjoys enthusiastic support from its union, held on to the world championship in 2002 and 2006.

Another exciting development for the women's game: The first Women's Rugby World Cup Sevens was played in Dubai in 2009, concurrent with the men's event. The Australian women's team took home the top prize.

1823
William Webb Ellis picks up the ball and runs with it.

1825
The first game of Australian "football" is played.

1841
Running with the ball is officially allowed in Rugby School. Rules provide that the ball must be caught on the bound (from a bouncing ball), the catcher must not be "off his side," and the catcher must not pass the ball.

1843
Guy's Hospital (London) Rugby Club formed.

1845
Football rulebook printed at Rugby School.

1848
The major public schools (Rugby, Eton, Harrow, Marlborough, Westminster, and Shrewsbury) meet to draw up the "Cambridge Rules."

1850
German rugby played for the first time at the Neuenheim College (now Heidelberg College). Students later form the *Heidelberger Ruderklub von 1872*, the oldest German rugby club.

Boys will be boys. *Courtesy of the World Rugby Museum.*

1854
Ireland's first rugby football club begins play at Dublin University.

1855
The earliest recorded game of rugby in the British Army (Guards vs. Cavalry) is played at Balaclava, in the midst of the Crimean War.

1857
Liverpool RFU, arguably the oldest continuously operating rugby club in the world, is founded.

Edinburgh Academy forms Scotland's first football club.

Blackheath Club is founded by old boys from the Blackheath Proprietary School.

1861
Montevideo Cricket Club, Uruguay, is the first club outside Europe to play rugby.

1862
First match is played in South Africa.

1863
Rugby and Association Football become separate entities. Rules are written for both sports and respective governing bodies are formed.

Australia's first club is formed at Sydney University.

1865
The first Canadian rugby game is played in Montreal between English regiment officers and civilians, mainly from McGill University.

1870
New Zealand's first game is played between Nelson College and Nelson football club. (The Nelson club wins 2–0.)

1871
The Rugby Football Union is founded at the Pall Mall

Restaurant in Regent Street, London.

The first international game, Scotland vs. England, is played at Raeburn Place in Edinburgh.

Neath, the first Welsh club, is formed.

Langholm Rugby Football Club, said to be Scotland's oldest, is formed.

1872

Le Havre, France's first club, is formed.

Oxford beats Cambridge in their first meeting, known ever after as "the Varsity match."

1873

Scottish RFU formed.

1874

On May 14, Harvard University hosts Montreal's McGill University at Cambridge, Massachusetts, in the first recorded rugby game on American soil.

First governing body, the New South Wales Rugby Union (NSWRU), also known as the Southern RU, formed in Australia.

1875

Two clubs, Hamilton and Villagers, are formed in South Africa. Both claim to be the oldest club in that country.

1876

International teams reduce their rosters from twenty to fifteen players.

Harvard, Yale, Princeton, and Columbia form the Intercollegiate Football Association.

1877

The Calcutta Cup is presented to the RFU.

1878

The first match under floodlights is played (Broughton vs. Swinton) on October 22 at Broughton's Yew Street ground in Salford, Greater Manchester.

1879

The two Irish Unions merge to become the Irish Rugby Football Union.

The first unions in New Zealand form in Canterbury and Wellington.

ENGLAND *v* SCOTLAND. *1871*

England's first international team. *Courtesy of the World Rugby Museum.*

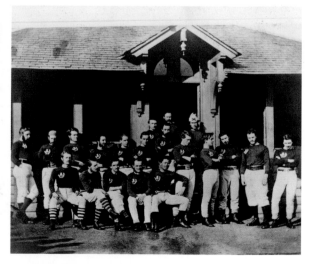

Scotland's first international team. *Courtesy of the World Rugby Museum.*

1880

Canadian RFU founded.

In the United States, the scrum is replaced by the line of scrimmage, signaling the move toward "American" football.

1881

The Welsh Rugby Union is founded.

1882

Queensland Rugby Union is founded.

New South Wales visits New Zealand, marking the first overseas tour. (The boat journey takes five days.)

1883

The first sevens tournament is played at Scotland's Melrose Football Club.

1886

The International Rugby Football Board (IRFB), later to become the IRB, is formed by Scotland, Wales, and Ireland.

1888

British team travels to Australia and New Zealand for the first major tour abroad.

1889

British Columbia Rugby Union and South African Rugby Football Board are formed.

1890

Wales beats England for the first time.

England becomes a member of the IRFB.

Player figurine, circa 1890. *Courtesy of the World Rugby Museum.*

1892

The New Zealand Rugby Football Union is formed.

1894

A "try" becomes worth 3 points and a conversion worth 2 points.

1895

Twenty-two leading clubs in Yorkshire and Lancashire break with the union and form the Northern Rugby Football Union (NRFU), which will become the Rugby League in 1922.

1900

Rugby is played for the first time at the second modern Olympic Games in Paris. (France wins the gold.)

1901

The Lancashire and Yorkshire factions of the Northern Rugby Football Union (NRFU) merge to become the Northern Rugby League. (This is the first time the name *Rugby League* is officially used.)

1905

New Zealand's first team, the All Blacks, tour the British Isles and beat Scotland, Ireland, and England.

1906

Players in the United States adopt the forward pass, once again moving away from rugby and toward American football.

1907

RFU committee member William Williams buys ten acres of land at Twickenham to be used for rugby. The site, nicknamed

"Billy's cabbage patch," was previously used to grow fruit trees, cabbages, and other vegetables.

1908
Australia wins gold at the London Olympics.

1909
The first German Club Championships are organized.

1910
First international is played at Twickenham. England beat Wales 11–6.

A team of rugby All-Americans, comprised of U.S. collegians, tours Australia and New Zealand.

1913
Fijian Rugby Union is founded.

1920
United States beats France (8–0) at Antwerp Olympics. (Only two teams compete.)

Fédération Française de Rugby formed.

1922
The Northern Rugby Football Union (NRFU) becomes the Rugby Football League.

1923
Spanish Rugby Federation founded.

Tongan RFU founded.

1924
United States beats France (17–3) to win gold at the Paris Olympics.

1926
Japanese RFU founded.

1928
Italian RFU founded.

1929
The Rugby Union of Canada is founded, lasting until the outbreak of the war in 1939. It is reestablished in 1965 as the Canadian Rugby Union.

1930
IRB takes responsibility for all changes in the *Laws of the Game*.

1931
New Zealand beats Australia (20–13) in the first-ever Bledisloe Cup.

1934
The FIRA (Federation of Amateur Rugby) is founded by Czechoslovakia, France, Germany, Holland, Italy, Portugal, Romania, Catalonia (Spain), and Sweden. (Belgium later joins.)

1938
The Calcutta Cup match between England and Scotland, played on March 19 at Twickenham, becomes the first international rugby game broadcast live on TV.

1939
War is declared and international rugby is suspended.

1948
Dropped goal reduced from 4 points to 3 points.

HATS OFF! In the early years of rugby, players were awarded beautifully embroidered wool caps when they played a match for their national union. Today, the term is mostly figurative. A player with thirty "caps" to his credit has played thirty prestigious national matches.

1949

The Australian Rugby Union is founded.

1950

Tom Brown's School Days filmed at Rugby School in Rugby, England.

1951

Uruguay Rugby Union is founded.

1959

The famous traveling club The Penguins is formed to promote the game and encourage friendship between countries.

1964

Georgian Rugby Union is founded.

1968

A provision for the replacement of injured players (up to two per team) is added to the *Laws*.

(Tactical substitutions and three replacements are introduced in 1996.)

1969

Wales wins three Grand Slams and six Triple Crowns.

All Black fullback, Fergie McCormick, scores a world-record 24 points in his side's 33–12 win over Wales in Auckland.

1971

Wales' John Taylor lands the most famous kick in Five Nations history when his left-footed conversion of Gerald Davies' corner try brings his team a 1-point win against Scotland.

1972

The Wales-New Zealand game becomes the first rugby match to be televised live by satellite back to New Zealand.

1974

Michael O'Brien becomes the first streaker at a major sporting event during the January England–France match at Twickenham.

1975

Four territorial organizations gather in Chicago to establish the United States of America Rugby Football Union (now known as USA Rugby).

1976

USA Rugby fields several national teams, all nicknamed the Eagles.

1982

First international women's match is played between France and the Netherlands in Utrecht.

1983

Women's Rugby Football Union (WRFU) is established to oversee rugby in England, Ireland, Scotland, and Wales. In 1994, each country forms its own governing body.

1984

The Wallabies become the first Australian team to win the Grand Slam in the seventy-six years since their first tour to the United Kingdom and Ireland.

1987

Australia and New Zealand co-host the first Rugby World Cup.

The USA Rugby Women's National Team is founded.

During the opening ceremony of the 1995 World Cup in South Africa, President Nelson Mandela wore a Springbok jersey, the uniform of the host country's team, which many people considered a symbol of the apartheid era. This gesture was seen as a dramatic invitation for the country to heal itself through sport.

1990

Scotland wins the Five Nations Championship, Grand Slam, and Triple Crown as well as the Calcutta Cup against England.

1991

The second Rugby World Cup is played in the United Kingdom, Ireland, and France.

The first (unofficial) Women's Rugby World Cup (WRWC) is played in Cardiff, Great Britain. The USA Eagles beat England 19–6 in the final.

1994

England wins the second unofficial WRWC, played in Edinburgh, Scotland.

The Rugby Football Union for Women (RFUW) is formed.

1995

The third Rugby World Cup is played in South Africa.

Rugby Union turns professional.

France's Philippe Sella, the first player to play in one hundred international matches plays his last international against England. (Jason Leonard surpasses the mark in 2003.)

1997

Laws committee introduces the white card and "sin-bin" (which later become yellow and red cards).

1998

The first official Women's Rugby World Cup is played in Amsterdam. New Zealand beats the United States in the final, 46–12.

The International Rugby Football Board drops the 'F' to become the IRB.

1999

Fourth Rugby World Cup is played in Wales.

2001

Celtic League Rugby begins play.

2002

New Zealand beats England (19–9) in Spain to win the second Women's Rugby World Cup.

The inaugural IRB Under-21 World Cup is played in South Africa. The host team, the Baby Boks, beats Australia in the final (24–21).

France becomes the first team to win a Grand Slam in the Six Nations Championship.

2003

England beats host country Australia to become the first Northern Hemisphere country to win the Rugby World Cup. The Wallabies score 17 points, the most ever scored by a losing side in a Rugby World Cup final.

2005

The inaugural IRB Under-19 Championships are played in Durban. South Africa beats New Zealand (20–15) to win the final.

2006

Women's Rugby World Cup is played in Edmonton, Canada. New Zealand wins again.

2007

During the Six Nations Championship, England's Jonny Wilkinson scores 228 points, surpassing the previous mark of 227 scored during the same competition, previously set by Scotland's Gavin Hastings. As of 2008, Wilkinson had scored a total of 1,023 points, including his world record 29 drop goals, along with 6 tries, 144 conversions, and 206 penalty goals.

3: THE RIGHT STUFF

All the Gear You Need to Play Rugby

One of the best things about rugby is the short equipment list. The only truly necessary item for a neighborhood pickup game is a ball. If it's an official match, the gear list (a "kit" in rugby jargon) grows a little more extensive: team jerseys, shorts, cleats, mouth guards, and a match ball. Still, compared to sports such as American football, rugby's requirements are minimal, making it inexpensive to play and accessible to all kinds of players all over the world.

HAVE A BALL

In rugby's early years, the early to mid-1800s, balls were made from pig's bladders that were blown up like balloons (courtesy of unlucky volunteers), knotted at the end, and covered with a leather casing. Balls were inconsistent in shape since each one took on the individual bladder's form. Then, in 1862, Richard Lindon, the boot and shoemaker credited with inventing the rugby ball (and, later, the brass hand pump), introduced rubber inner tubes, which were more pliable than the pig bladders, thus changing the ball's shape from a sphere or a pear shape to a more consistent oval or egg shape.

As legend has it, early rugby players wanted an oval ball to distinguish their game from the round ball used in soccer. Whatever the motivation, in 1892, the RFU made it official and mandated oval balls for all matches. Ever-improving technology allowed manufacturers to follow these guidelines and make their products uniform.

The distinctive rugby oval.

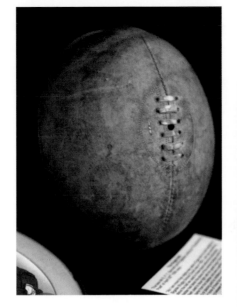

Game ball, circa 1851. *Courtesy of the Rugby Museum.*

THE MODERN OVAL

For decades, most rugby balls were encased in leather, which meant they could become very heavy in wet conditions. By the 1980s, balls were almost universally covered in synthetic, waterproof material, for which ballcarriers have been eternally grateful. Plus, the rules allow for balls to be chemically treated to make them water resistant and easier to grip.

The pill, the oval, *le ballon*... by any name, rugby balls today come in two types. Match balls are high-quality, well-balanced, game-ready balls, while training balls are less expensive versions of the real deal, best for using at home or at practice.

John Batchelor has been hand-stitching balls in Rugby, England, for more than forty years.

According to the *Laws of the Game,* here are the requirements for match balls:

Shape:

■ *Ball must be oval and made of four panels.*

Dimensions:

■ *Length in line: 280–300 millimeters [11–12 in]*

■ *Circumference (end to end): 740–770 millimeters [29–30 in]*

■ *Circumference (in width): 580–620 millimeters [23–24 in]*

Materials:

■ *Leather or suitable synthetic material. It may be treated to make it water resistant and easier to grip.*

■ *Weight: 410–460 grams [14–16 oz]*

■ *Air Pressure at the Start of Play: 65.71 kilopascals, or 0 .67–0.70 kilograms per square centimeter, or 9.5–10.0 pounds per square inch.*

Note: Spare balls may be used during matches as long as teams do not attempt to gain an unfair advantage by using them or changing them. Also, smaller balls may be used for matches between young players.

TIP FOR PLAYERS

■ Buy a ball (and pump) of your own to practice at home. The more you touch and get comfortable with the ball, the better you'll play.

■ Check online stores for the best selection of rugby balls.

■ Make sure the ball is properly inflated but still has enough "give" for you to grip it easily.

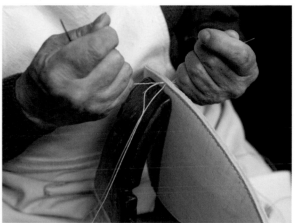

The tradition of hand-stitching balls continues to this day.

AIR MATTERS

Q: Why does the air come out of the ends of the ball when I inflate it?

A: The air that escapes from the ends of the ball when it is inflated comes from between the bladder and the inner facing surface of the ball. This is NOT the air that is being pumped into the ball; it is air that is trapped between the

bladder and inner facing. This is a natural occurrence and doesn't necessarily mean that the ball is punctured or has faulty valves.

Q: How much do I pump up a ball, and how long does it stay inflated?

A: Rugby balls have a recommended psi (pounds per square inch) of between

8 and 10. Balls that are not inflated to this pressure will suffer in their performance, not traveling as far or as fast as properly inflated balls. If balls are overinflated, they will be out of shape and the stitching will become exposed and stretched. Balls should be reinflated or topped up after a week or so.

—from http://www.gilbert-rugby.com

TO A TEE

Most kicks are made by hand (the kicker holds the ball, lets it drop, then lets it fly). But certain types of kicks at goal call for the ball to be placed before the kicker has at it. Before tees, the only option for goal kickers was to hold the ball in place with sand prior to kicking conversions or penalty kicks. Some still employ this method, despite the fact that waiting for a ball boy to carry a bucket of sand from the sideline to the field and create a mound for the ball can be pretty tedious. Plus, sand is not very effective when it's raining. These days, most kickers use kicking tees, the small, round, plastic devices that sit on the ground and hold the ball upright. These are the same tees used by gridiron football kickers during kickoffs.

TIP FOR PLAYERS

If you aspire to be a successful goal kicker, then buy a tee (they're inexpensive) to practice with at home. Then, outside practice, you can take your time and experiment with kicking the ball from different angles.

SUIT UP

During the first rugby games, English schoolboys hit the pitch en masse, wearing their regular school clothes and shoes, although they did manage to fling off their ties, jackets, and top hats prior to match time. Soon, schools and clubs sought out uniforms to separate themselves from their opponents and of course, to look good during matches. Assigning players numbers according to their position came later still.

PERIOD COSTUME

1839—The Rugby school team is the first to adopt a uniform, consisting of red velvet caps, white trousers, and jerseys in the color of each player's choice.

1871—At the first international rugby match, the English players wear all white with a red rose on their jerseys, while the Scots sport blue shirts and cricket flannels.

1875—The Harvard-Yale game marks the first time uniforms are worn in an American "football" game. Yale wears dark trousers, blue shirts, and yellow caps. Harvard wears crimson shirts, stockings, and knee breeches.

1921—The IRB introduces numbering on jerseys.

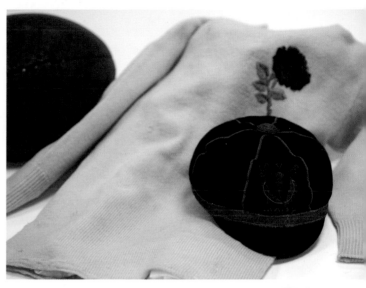

England's first official uniform. *Courtesy of the World Rugby Museum.*

ON TOP

Rugby jerseys are an icon of the sport, popularized by top international pro teams and Ivy League college teams in the United States. Fans who never spent a minute on the pitch have been known to sport boldly striped heavy cotton shirts made by Ralph Lauren or Calvin Klein.

Many teams still wear traditional cotton jerseys, which look great but are very hot and tend to get soaked during a game. (This is why during tournaments you'll often see jerseys laid out across the grass drying out between games.) More and more teams are adopting jerseys made from microfiber fabrics that wick sweat away from the skin and dry quickly. Whatever they're made of, rugby jerseys should be sturdy, both for practice and for game day.

Jerseys laid out to dry.

In international competition, it has long been the tradition for players to swap jerseys after matches. Although players still do this, the practice may be waning a bit in the era of eBay.

DOWN LOW

Like jerseys, rugby shorts are best made of tough, functional, breathable material. Players are wise to choose shorts that are comfortable, but not too loose. (No need to give an opponent too much fabric for a handhold.) Drawstrings are preferable to elastic when it comes to waistbands, as any player whose shorts have been pulled down during a maul will confirm. The one thing not allowed: shorts with padding sewn into them.

Note: Many coaches ask their players to wear uniform shorts, warm-up t-shirts, and exercise sandals to the field on game day. The team changes into uniform jerseys, socks, shin guards, and rugby shoes just prior to game time.

BOOT UP

Rugby shoes, or "boots," are a player's key piece of equipment. Although running shoes or other athletic shoes are fine for kids playing a neighborhood pickup game, they're discouraged on the pitch and even against the rules in some leagues.

Like most athletic footwear, rugby shoes have come a long way in terms of materials and technology. Until the 1940s, most playing shoes were made from unwaterproofed leather that became heavy and unwieldy on a wet field. Today, the world's top players seek out shoes with microfiber uppers, to keep the foot dry, and components such as lace covers, which increase the area of contact when kicking the ball.

Shoes, or cleats, come in every imaginable color these days, but black is probably the most popular color for players worldwide. Some clubs have rules regarding the color of shoes to be worn, since shoes are part of the uniform. Ditto for socks.

STEP BY STEP

Rugby boots come in several varieties: low, medium, or high-cut and soft or hard toe.

When it comes to boots, go all-black (or almost).

Many players choose their shoes based on their position. For example, most backs prefer soft-toe boots so they can feel the ball when kicking. Forwards, who are most likely to get stepped on, usually choose hard-toe boots.

As for the cut, backs often prefer low (for speed and changing direction) while forwards often opt for medium (which give more support for close contact work). For maximum ankle support, high-cut is the way to go.

Just to complicate matters, shoes are *further* classified by field conditions: turf shoes (best for artificial surfaces or hard, compacted fields), firm ground shoes (good on soft and hard outdoor fields), and soft ground shoes (made for soft field conditions).

Pros and national team players often keep several pairs of shoes on hand. If you're just starting out or can only afford one pair, go for firm ground shoes.

A comfortable fit is the most important consideration. Don't wear shoes that are too tight or too big—blisters make players miserable. Ultimately, let your personal preference be your guide.

BOOT-LESS: Some players actually forgo the boots and play rugby barefoot. You'll see this in beach rugby games in the United States and Australia. Also, very young players in South Africa often play barefoot so they won't hurt each other with their shoes.

Studs

The studs (also called sprigs) on rugby boots are similar to those on soccer or football cleats, except that the studs must be circular and otherwise meet IRB regulations. Molded rubber multi-studded soles are acceptable provided they have no sharp edges or ridges, but toe studs (like those on football cleats) are not allowed. A variety of stud patterns are available, and players should select according to the needs of their positions. It may take some trial and error to determine which shoes give the best traction.

The underside of rugby.

Tip for Players

- When buying boots for the first time, ask a coach or a teammate for advice.
- Before buying online, where the selection is the best, try on shoes at a sporting goods store or at a rugby tournament, where vendors often sell boots.
- Always clean your boots after the match, especially if the field was muddy. Let the leather dry out before the next match.

Socks

The last thing a jumper or a lifter wants to worry about during a line-out is his socks. Rugby socks, traditionally worn to the knee, need to stay up and in place. For decades, players wore socks made of cotton or wool and tied strings around them at the knee to prevent them from falling down. This was less than effective. Today's socks are made of spandex or other moisture-repelling material (sometimes even anti-microbial!) and stay put courtesy of built-in elastic at the cuff and ankle.

Rugby socks are a distinctive part of a player's uniform—the field comes alive with all those multi-colored stripes on top of busy feet.

Socks should stay put.

Game ready.

KIT BAG

Every player needs a bag to stow her stuff and tote it to and from the field. Many clubs furnish team bags. If you need to purchase your own, make sure it's tough and lightweight and has a separate, preferably waterproof, compartment for wet, sweaty stuff. Keep all your equipment in your kit bag, along with a towel, a water bottle, and a change of clothes. You may also want to include a few first aid items such as band-aids, adhesive tape, and gauze pads.

PROTECTION

Safety should be everyone's priority on the pitch, and rugby's rough-and-tumble requires some special preparations. The *Laws of the Game* is very specific regarding what protective equipment is and is not allowed. (Always check the most recent version of the *Laws,* as this section is constantly evolving.) The IRB's website (http://www.irb.com) lists approved equipment by manufacturer, in case you're wondering what brand to buy. The "Regulations" section of the *Laws* lists the exact thickness, density, measurements, and other specifications of permitted equipment.

MOUTH GUARDS

In rugby, your mouth is bound to get hit or bumped by someone or something at some point. When it does, you'll be glad to have protection for your teeth. Most pros and almost every youth and college

Inspiration: Sharon Whitehead, who plays the position of loosehead prop on England's Women's Team and grew up in a rugby league family, used to polish her uncle's boots with bacon grease when she was seven years old.

Watch your mouth.

player wear mouth guards or dental protectors. In many leagues, especially youth leagues, mouth guards are mandatory. Purchase guards from a dentist or from a sporting goods store. (Football mouth guards are fine.)

HEADGEAR

Headgear is allowed, provided it's made of thin, soft material and bears the IRB approval mark. Not all players wear it, but the trend is moving toward more players donning caps. Some players nix headgear because it's too hot. Others won't play without it, especially those looking to protect their ears.

SHOULDER PADS

Players may wear shoulder pads made of thin, soft material that fit under an undergarment or jersey. The pads must cover the shoulder and collarbone only. Highly recommended.

Heads up!

CHEST PADS

In addition to shoulder pads, women may wear chest pads made of thin, soft material that cover the shoulder, collarbone, and/or chest. Most women ruggers also wear good, supportive sports bras, with or without chest pads.

SHIN GUARDS

Players may wear lightly padded shin guards under their socks. Shin guards should fit snugly, but comfortably, extending from just below the knee to two or three inches above the ankle.

MITTS

Fingerless gloves or mitts of stretch material are allowed as long as they don't cover the fingers and thumbs beyond the outer

Gotcha covered.

joint or extend beyond the wrist. No buttons or potentially dangerous parts are permitted on the gloves.

Compression Shorts

Both men and women may wear compression shorts for extra support. Some men prefer to wear jock straps. Choose the most comfortable option for you.

X-tra Protection

Players are permitted to wear thin tape (on ankles, knees, elbows) for extra support. Also allowed: bandages, dressings, or braces (provided they are soft, with no metal parts) to cover or protect injuries.

No-No's

For safety reasons, some things simply may not be worn on the field:

- Any item contaminated by blood

- Any sharp or abrasive item

- Anything containing buckles, clips, rings, hinges, zippers, screws, bolts, or rigid material or projection

- Jewelry such as rings or earrings

- Communication devices within a player's clothing or attached to the body

- Anything else, even items normally permitted, that the referee decides might be dangerous

Coach's Checklist

Coaches will want to keep some additional equipment on hand, including:

- A pump (to inflate balls)

- A first-aid kit

- Water

- Traffic cones (to use for drills and/or makeshift goals)

- A set of scrimmage vests

- Kicking tees

Better-funded teams may want to consider:

- Tackle bags (large foam-filled bags that players hit during tackling drills)

- Rucking pads (wedge-shaped pads with handles to use during contact drills)

- Contact suits (padded suits players wear during tackling drills)

- Scrum machine (a hydraulic scrum-simulating sled; budget $1200–$10,000)

4: How to Play Rugby

From Set-Up to Set Pieces

Rugby may be the most egalitarian sport around. Players of different physiques, skills, and ages are all encouraged to play. Everybody plays offense. Everybody plays defense. Everyone gets the ball. Everyone has a chance to score. Both women and men play the exact same game. And what's not to like about a game where points are awarded for a try?

> As the saying goes, in rugby, the forwards decide who wins a match and the backs decide by how much.

THE FIELD OF PLAY

In rugby, the playing area is a rectangle that comprises the field of play and the in-goal areas. The most important requirement for a rugby pitch is that it be safe. Usually, the surface is grass, but sand, clay, snow, and artificial turf are allowed as well. Coaches and referees should always check the playing surface for rocks, glass, and holes prior to a practice or match. Other safeguards, such as padding for the goalposts, should be put in place for game day.

Here's how the *Laws of the Game* defines each part of the pitch:

- *The Field of Play: the area between the goal lines and the touchlines. These lines are not part of the field of play.*
- *The Playing Area: the field of play and the in-goal areas. The touchlines, touch-in-goal lines and dead ball lines are not part of the playing area.*
- *The Playing Enclosure: the playing area and a space around it, not less than 5 meters where practicable, which is known as the perimeter area.*
- *In-goal: the area between the goal line and the dead ball line, and between the touch-in-goal lines. It includes the goal line but it does not include the dead ball line or the touch-in-goal lines.*
- *The 22: the area between the goal line and the 22-meter line, including the 22-meter line but excluding the goal line.*

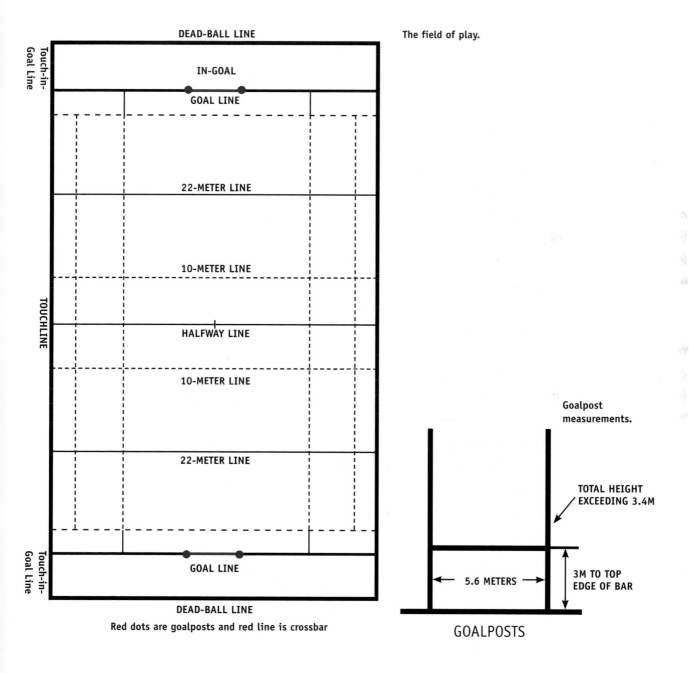

The field of play.

DEAD-BALL LINE

IN-GOAL

GOAL LINE

22-METER LINE

10-METER LINE

HALFWAY LINE

10-METER LINE

22-METER LINE

GOAL LINE

DEAD-BALL LINE

Touch-in-Goal Line

TOUCHLINE

Touch-in-Goal Line

Red dots are goalposts and red line is crossbar

Goalpost measurements.

TOTAL HEIGHT EXCEEDING 3.4M

5.6 METERS

3M TO TOP EDGE OF BAR

GOALPOSTS

Here are the dimensions the *Laws* specifies for field and goalposts:

- *The field of play does not exceed 100 meters [109.4 yd] in length and 70 meters [76.6 yd] in width. Each in-goal does not exceed 22 meters [24 yd] in length and 70 meters [76.6 yd] in width.*
- *The distance between the goal posts is 5.6 meters [6.1 yd]. The crossbar is placed between the two goal posts so that its top edge is 3.0 meters [3.3 yd] from the ground.*
- *The minimum height of the goal posts is 3.4 meters [3.7 yd].*

LINES

To new players, the lines on a rugby field can look like a crosshatch of confusion. Here is a quick read between the lines:

HALFWAY LINE: A solid line marking the middle of the field where play starts and restarts after successful tries, drop goals, or penalty goals.

5-METER LINE: One of two broken lines that run between try lines, parallel to the touchlines, marking the front of the line-out and the minimum distance a throw-in must travel.

10-METER LINE: One of two broken lines located 10 meters (10.9 yd) on either side of the halfway line, marking the point the ball must reach for a kickoff to be legal.

22-METER LINE: One of two solid lines located 22 meters (24 yd) from each goal line. Drop-outs (drop-kicks used to restart play) are taken from behind these lines. Players' positions relative to this line determine the course of many plays.

GOAL LINE (OR TRY LINE): The solid line at each end of the field of play marking the beginning of the in-goal area. Players must reach this line to score a try.

DEAD-BALL LINE: The line past the in-goal area at each end of the field marking the point where the ball is called out of play.

TOUCHLINE: One of two solid lines that run vertically between goal lines (think of the sidelines in soccer or football). When the ball makes contact with the touchline or moves past it, it is said to be "in touch" or out of bounds.

TOUCH-IN-GOAL LINE: The extension of the touchline between the goal line and the dead-ball line.

DASH LINES: Besides the major lines mentioned above, the field is also marked with 1-meter (1.1 yd) dash lines, which provide reference points for referees and players in situations such as scrums, line-outs, and penalty kicks. Included are the following:

- 15-meter dash lines: Located 15 meters (16.4 yd) in and parallel to each touchline, these seven lines intersect the goal lines, the 22-meter lines, the 10-meter lines, and the halfway line.

- 5-meter dash lines: Six 5-meter dash lines are marked 5 meters (5.5 yd) in front of and parallel to each try line away from the touchline at 5 meters (5.5 yd), 15 meters (16.4 yd), and in front of each goalpost.

- Halfway dash line: This 0.5-meter-long (0.5 yd) dash line intersects the halfway line at midfield and marks the spot where kickoffs and restarts originate.

FLAGS

There are fourteen flags on the rugby pitch (each with a minimum height of 1.2 meters [1.3 yd] above the ground), which mark the following:

Flags on the pitch.

- Intersections of the dead-ball and touch-in-goal lines
- The three-way intersection of the goal lines, touchlines, and touch-in-goal lines
- The 22-meter and halfway lines

TIP FOR COACHES

For some clubs, especially new ones without pitches of their own, one of the biggest challenges is finding practice space and game fields. If a coach doesn't take on the task himself, he should designate someone to reserve fields ahead of time and double-check their availability the day before or day of a match or practice. Don't assume you can show up on a municipal field and find space. You'll sometimes have to make do with soccer and football fields. On the upside, rugby can easily be played in these borrowed spaces.

The team can practice on an unmarked field, but coaches should bring flags and cones to designate boundaries. For games on non-rugby pitches, plan ahead for marking the field, and don't forget the flags and cones!

WHAT'S THE POINT?

According to the *Laws of the Game,* the objective in rugby is for two 15-man teams each to attempt to score as many points as possible by carrying, passing, kicking, and grounding the ball. The team that scores the most points wins.

According to the long and storied tradition of the sport, all this should be carried out in a sporting spirit while observing fair play.

"This is a gentleman's game," says Michael Badger, founder of the Valley Forge Rugby Club in Pennsylvania. "We play hard, then shake hands. We respect each other as athletes."

OBJECTIVE: PLAY RUGBY

According to the *Laws of the Game*, here's how a rugby match is played:

- *A match is started by a kick-off.*

- *After the kick-off, any player who is onside may take the ball and run with it.*

- *Any player may throw the ball or kick it.*

- *Any player may give the ball to another player.*

- *Any player may tackle, hold, or push an opponent holding the ball.*

- *Any player may fall on the ball.*

- *Any player may take part in a scrum, ruck, maul, or line-out.*

- *Any player may ground the ball in-goal.*

Of course, all of the above must be done in accordance with the *Laws of the Game*.

POSSESSION AND CONTINUITY

Rugby is all about the contest for possession of the ball and the challenge of continuously moving it toward the goal in order to score. Players compete for possession during general play, as well as when play is restarted after a score or a foul or when the ball goes out of bounds. (The restart may take the form of a kick or one of rugby's characteristic "set piece" formations, the line-out and the scrum.)

When a team gains possession of the ball, the idea is to maintain possession, keep the ball away from the opposing team, and advance the ball down the field. This is done by running with the ball, kicking it, or passing to a teammate. Since this is rugby, the ball's progress may be marked by the backward pass, the offensive tackle, and other distinctive components of the game, including rucks and mauls—groups of players that form to contest possession after a player is tackled. We'll look more closely at these characteristic moves in the next chapter.

The goal of advancing the ball sounds easy enough, but here's the wrinkle: While the attacking team attempts to move the ball downfield, the opposing team is working hard to tackle the ballcarrier and steal the ball away. If the defense is successful, they immediately switch to attack mode and attempt to move the ball downfield the other way and score for themselves. And so it goes.

A player possessed.

TIME

Rugby matches are played for two 40-minute halves for a total of 80 minutes. After the 10-minute halftime break, teams switch sides of the field.

The game clock runs continuously unless the referee makes the call to stop the clock for injury, the substitution of players, foul play, or some other incident. For example, the ref might call a halt on account of bad weather (lightning) or to give a player a chance to replace a bloody or badly torn jersey.

At halftime, players take a much-needed break.

Note: Match times may vary according to the rules of individual unions. Under-19 matches usually consist of two 35-minute halves. Games may run shorter but may not exceed a total of 70 minutes for this age group.

START

Matches begin with a kickoff, taken at the halfway line. Players on the nonkicking team must line up behind their own 10-meter line. Players on the kicking team must remain behind the ball until it is struck. The ball must reach the nonkicking team's 10-meter line for the kick to be legal. Once it is in play, both teams compete for possession.

If the ball is kicked off directly into touch (out of bounds) or into the opponent's in-goal area, the nonkicking team may choose to redo the kickoff, take a line-out at the halfway line, or have a scrum at midfield. (Most teams choose the scrum since it's a better attacking opportunity.)

TIP FOR TEAM CAPTAINS

The winner of the coin toss (taken by the team captains) can greatly benefit his team when he chooses which goal to defend. Check out the direction of the wind and the sun to give your side the edge.

Note: The captain also chooses whether to kick off or receive the ball. If he chooses to kick off, the other team will do so when the game resumes after halftime.

NOW WHAT?

Any player on either team may advance the ball down the field by running with it, passing it, or kicking it. It's rare for a player to run all the way to the goal line without getting tackled, so from their first day on the pitch, players need to learn to pass so that the ball may carry on when they go down.

Pass backwards or sideways only.

"It doesn't matter who scores, only that we score."—LARRY GELWIX, COACH OF HIGHLAND RUGBY CLUB, SEVENTEEN-TIME NATIONAL HIGH SCHOOL CHAMPS FEATURED IN THE 2008 MOVIE *FOREVER STRONG*.

DOGGONE IT

At sporting events, it's not unusual to see the occasional stray dog run onto the field. But in an 1890s match between Portsmouth Victoria and Southampton Trojans, a ball kicked into the Trojans' in-goal area rebounded off a dog, and one of the Portsmouth players gathered the ball and claimed a try. The Trojans protested. But since the ball had rebounded off a dog and not off a spectator, the try stood.

Rule #1 in rugby: No Forward Passing. (The rugby term for an illegal forward pass is a *knock-on*.) The ball must always be thrown either *laterally* or *backward*. According to the *Laws of the Game*, a pass that is thrown backward but hits the ground and bounces forward is legal. A backward pass that is blown forward is also legal. It's not these accidents of nature that refs are watching; it's what the players do with the ball.

The last option to elude defenders and advance the ball toward the goal is kicking. Booting the ball is a task most often relegated to backs, but, like everything else in rugby, it can be any player's game.

SCORE!

In rugby, points are added to the scoreboard in several ways. The highest-scoring maneuver is a "try," worth 5 points. A try is scored when a runner carries the ball over the opposing goal line and places it down on the ground. Following a successful try, the scoring team may attempt a conversion kick (2 points) by kicking the ball over the crossbar of the goalposts from the point where the try was scored.

A team may also be awarded 5 points for a penalty try. This occurs when the referee rules that the defending team committed a foul that prevented what would surely have been a successful try.

Teams may also score by taking a free kick (3 points) following a penalty or kicking a dropped goal (3 points) from the field. (See Chapter 5.)

Following any type of score, the nonscoring team kicks off to the scoring team to restart the match.

STARTS AND RESTARTS

Although continuity is the goal in the free-flowing game of rugby, sometimes play must be stopped because of a foul, a ball going out of bounds, or a score. Players start or restart matches via kickoffs, scrums, line-outs, throw-ins, penalty kicks, and free kicks.

The ultimate goal.

KICKOFF: Used to begin the match or restart play after halftime or following a score. One player from the kicking team drop-kicks the ball from the center of the halfway line. Both teams then compete for possession of the ball.

SCRUM: Used to restart play after certain minor infractions, the scrum is a contest in which eight players from each side bind together (each player firmly grasping another player's body from the shoulder to the hips, using his entire arm, from hand to shoulder) and push against each other in an attempt to gain possession of the ball with their feet.

LINE-OUTS: Used to restart play after the ball, or a player carrying the ball, goes out of bounds. Players from both teams line up across from each other. Then one player from the restarting team (the team that did not last throw, kick, or have possession of the ball when it went into touch) throws the ball down the middle of the "tunnel" between the opposing rows of players and both teams compete for possession.

THROW-IN: A player on the restarting team may restart play by taking a quick throw-in (surprising the other team) without waiting for a line-out to form. This may only be done if the line-out has not yet formed, and the ball must travel at least 5 meters (5.5 yd).

PENALTY KICKS/FREE KICKS: Kicks on goal taken by the nonoffending team after an infringement by the opponent.

> Back in 1978, at Cardiff, Wales, the team developed a short pass to one of the halfbacks who would then go charging ahead with the ball. He became known as the "flying half back," which over time got shortened to "fly half."

CATCH-22

The 22-meter lines are more than just the points marking 22 meters (24 yd) in front of each goal line and the points from which restart kicks (drop-outs) are made. The two lines (along with the area of the field between the 22 and the goal lines, known as the 22 area) are very important strategic locations on the pitch.

For instance, if a kicker boots the ball directly into touch from on or behind her own 22-meter line, a line-out will be formed from where the ball crossed the line, allowing the attacking team a chance to gain territory. But if the kicker boots the ball directly into touch from in front of her own 22-meter line, the line-out will be formed from where the ball was kicked, which could cause her team to lose territory.

When it comes time to take the drop-out, the kicking team has several strategies to employ on or around the 22-meter line, such as drop-kicking the ball just over the line and regathering it immediately, or kicking it directly into touch, in which case the receiving team will either take another drop-out or choose to form a scrum or line-out at the 22-meter line.

GET IN POSITION

Rugby is played with fifteen players on each side. Ideally, a team will have at least twenty-two players on its roster to allow for tactical substitutions and replacement of injured players during the match.

In fledgling rugby leagues, it's often a challenge to recruit fifteen players, let alone twenty-two. Fortunately, the *Laws* allows for unions to authorize matches played with fewer than fifteen players per team. This is fairly common in the youth game. When teams play with fewer players, the *Laws* states that each side must have five players in the scrum at all times. (As we'll shortly see, only certain players form the scrum.)

Ready for action.

Experienced rugby coaches concur that young players often thrive on smaller teams. Of course, rugby sevens is always an option. For the standard game, adjustments in field dimensions, ball size, number of players, and duration of the match may be made according to the players' age. *Rugby: Steps to Success,* an excellent guide for youth coaches, makes the following recommendations:

AGE	PITCH SIZE	NUMBER OF PLAYERS	BALL SIZE	DURATION OF PLAY
Under 7	30m × 20m (32.8 × 21.9 yd)	5–7	3	Two 10min. halves
Under 8	30m × 20m (32.8 × 21.9 yd)	5–7	3	Two 10-min. halves
Under 9	50m × 35m (54.7 × 38.3 yd)	9 (3 forwards, 6 backs)	3	Two 10-min. halves
Under 10	50m × 35m (54.7 × 38.3 yd)	9 (3 forwards, 6 backs)	3	Two 15-min. halves
Under 11	59m × 38m (64.5 × 41.6 yd)	9 (3 forwards, 6 backs)	3	Two 15-min. halves
Under 12	59m × 43m (64.5 × 47.0 yd)	12 (5 forwards, 7 backs)	4	Two 20-min. halves
Under 13	59m × 43m (64.5 × 47.0 yd)	12 (5 forwards, 7 backs)	4	Two 20-min. halves
Under 14	Full size	15 (8 forwards, 7 backs)	4	Two 25-min. halves
Under 15	Full size	15 (8 forwards, 7 backs)	5	Two 30-min. halves
Over 15	Full size	15 (8 forwards, 7 backs)	5	Two 35-min. halves
Over 19	Full size	15 (8 forwards, 7 backs)	5	Two 40-min. halves

Note: In the U-19 game, if a team is made up of twenty-two players or more, it must include at least six players who can play in the front row so replacements are available for the positions of loose-head prop, hooker, and tight-head prop. There must also be three players who can play in lock position.

THE PLAYERS

Although every player on a side performs many of the same duties—running, tackling, kicking, handling the ball—specialized positions are still a critical part of the game. Almost every rugger plays more than one position over the course of his career, but as a rule, players are placed in their position according to skills and body type. (Forwards: big and strong. Backs: fast and agile.)

In general, the fifteen players on a side consist of eight forwards (the pack) and seven backs (the back line).

Call in the reserves.

By the Numbers

On the rugby pitch, a player's number indicates his on-field job. Here's a breakdown:

NUMBER(S)	POSITION(S)
1	Loose-head prop
2	Hooker
3	Tight-head prop
4, 5	Locks
6	Blindside flanker
7	Openside flanker
8	Number 8
9	Scrumhalf
10	Flyhalf
11	Left wing
12	Inside center
13	Outside center
14	Right wing
15	Fullback

There are also names for certain groupings of position players. In orderly rugby fashion, these are also listed by the numbers:

1, 2, 3, 4, 5, 6, 7, 8	Forwards
1, 2, 3	Front row (front rowers)
1, 2, 3, 4, 5	Front five (tight five)
4, 5	Second row (second rowers)
6, 7, 8	Back row (back rowers)
9, 10, 11, 12, 13, 14, 15	Backs
11, 14, 15	Back three
11, 12, 13, 14, 15	Back five

Note: The numbers above (1 through 15) are for the starting players. As a rule, the reserves (who come in as substitutes during the game) are numbered 16 through 22. Also, position names vary, depending on which part of the world you call home and which brand of the game you play. The names we're using here are the most common rugby union terms.

Forwards

The main objective of the forwards (two props, the hooker, two locks, two flankers, and the number 8) is to win possession of the ball. These eight players (who wear numbers 1 through 8) are the ones who form the scrum, and they may be further classified into three groups according to their positions in it: front row, second row, and back row.

The three front row players (numbers 1 through 3) and the two second row players (numbers 4 and 5) who line up behind them are nicknamed "the tight five." Their job? To keep the scrum steady and gain possession. Here are more detailed descriptions for these positions:

Tight Five

LOOSE-HEAD PROP (#1): Big, strong player. Responsible for scrumming in the front row and lifting jumpers (who leap for the ball) in the line-out.

HOOKER (#2): Strong, skilled player. Hooks the ball with his foot during the scrum and throws in at line-outs.

TIGHT-HEAD PROP (#3): The anchor of the scrum. She packs in directly opposite where the scrumhalf puts the ball in.

LOCKS (#4, #5): Tall players with "good hands." Responsible for taking restarts and jumping for the ball in the line-out.

Back Row

BLINDSIDE FLANKER (#6): Powerful player with great ball-handling skills. Binds onto the scrum on the blind side (the short side of the field).

OPENSIDE FLANKER (#7): Dynamic player. Critical to defense. Responsible for making tackles and creating turnovers.

NUMBER EIGHT: (#8): Pivotal player. Directs the scrum from the rear.

Note: Since players in the back row are expected to quickly retrieve loose balls, they are also called "loosies."

The number 8s and the halfbacks touch the ball more times during a match than any other players.

Backs

The main objective of the backs (scrumhalf, flyhalf, two wings, two centers, and a fullback) is to move the ball downfield and score. These seven players (who wear numbers 9 through 15) may be further classified into two groups: the back three and the back five, referring to their field position during the scrum.

Here are more detailed descriptions for these positions:

Back Three

SCRUMHALF (#9): Compact, quick player. Sometimes called the "halfback," he's responsible for great passes and maneuvering in tight spaces. Special skill: low-to-the-ground passes from the scrum.

FLYHALF (#10): Fast player, quick thinker. Runs, passes, and kicks.

LEFT WING (#11): One of the fastest players. Frequently kicks on offense and quickly switches to defensive mode.

The left wing switches to D.

Back Five

INSIDE CENTER (#12): Quick, powerful player. Responsible for running the ball and tackling.

OUTSIDE CENTER (#13): Fast runner, great ball handler. Responsible for running the ball and defending.

RIGHT WING (#14): One of the fastest players. Frequently kicks on offense and quickly switches to defensive mode.

FULLBACK (#15): Strong, tactical player. Capable of long, accurate kicks and aggressive running.

VIEW FROM THE SIDELINES

"One of the great things about rugby is that it takes a portfolio of body types. You need some short people because the ball is low to the ground, and a person built low to the ground can pick it up and put it in play easier. You need some tall, thin athletes that have good aerial skills and can win a contest for possession high off the ground. And you need some people that are built like mailboxes, without any connecting parts, because there are some aspects of the game where there's power and force and pushing and driving becomes important. It's rare in a sport that so many different body types are required."—*Cal Rugby coach Jack Clark*

Reserves

When a player is injured, the referee will call for him to be replaced. Once replaced, the player may not return to the match. The exception is when a bleeding player is temporarily replaced until the bleeding stops, after which he may come back in.

Substitutions are made for tactical reasons, most often to give tired players a break by bringing in reinforcements. According to the *Laws of the Game*:

- *If a player is substituted, that player must not return and play in that match even to replace an injured player.*
- *Exception 1: a substituted player may replace a player with a bleeding or open wound.*
- *Exception 2: a substituted player may replace a front row player when injured, temporarily suspended or sent off.*

Sending in reserve players with particular skills is an exact science at the higher level of the game. For safety purposes, the *Laws* further specifies the need for a set number of experienced players in certain positions. It's important for coaches to familiarize themselves with this list of requirements.

ON AND OFF

Almost as important as what players do is where exactly on the field they do it. The concept of onside and offside is a key element in rugby, and more complicated than in many other sports. Players are required to be onside at all times on all parts of the field. This holds true for both attackers and defenders during general play as well as during set pieces (scrums and line-outs).

In general play, a player is offside if he is in front of a teammate who is carrying the ball or if he is in front of the teammate who last played the ball. Basically, to remain onside, both offensive and defensive players should strive to remain on their team's side of the ball.

Action/Reaction

It's not unusual for a player to become offside (and considered temporarily out of the game) at any point during a match. When he does, the player should do his best to get behind the ball so he can get back in the game and avoid a penalty. In some cases, the actions of other players (intentionally or unintentionally) switch a player's status from off- to onside.

A player is back onside when:

- He runs behind the ballcarrier or the teammate who last kicked, touched, or carried the ball.
- The ballcarrier runs past him in the direction of the opponent's goal.

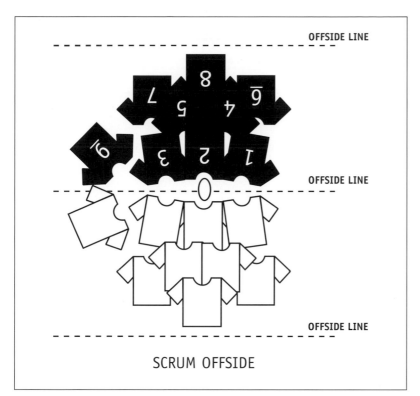

SCRUM OFFSIDE

Players must remain onside at all times in the scrum and the line-out. *Courtesy of USA Rugby.*

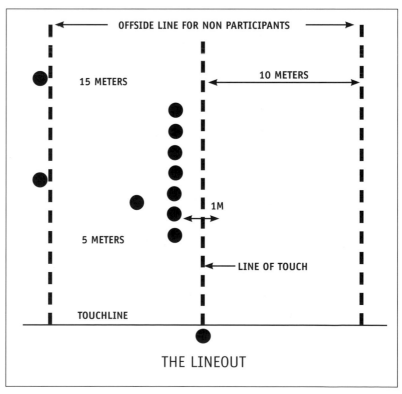

THE LINEOUT

Strive to stay onside at all times.

- A teammate who has kicked the ball forward runs in front of him.

- An opponent carrying the ball runs downfield 5 meters (5.5 yd).

- An opponent kicks or passes the ball.

- An opponent touches the ball but does not catch it.

A player is penalized for being offside only if he:

- Interferes with play

- Moves forward toward the ball

■ Fails to comply with the 10-meter law, which prohibits a player in an offside position from going within 10 meters (10.9 yd) of where the opponent is waiting to play the ball

Note: A player is considered accidentally offside if he can't avoid being touched by the ball or by a teammate carrying the ball. If his team gets no benefit from his offside position, play is not stopped. If his team does benefit from his offside position, the ref calls for a scrum, with the opposing team putting in the ball.

Offside during Contact

Players must attempt to remain onside at all times, even during the confusion of a tackle, ruck, or maul.

During a ruck, when two or more players from each team are in contact competing for the ball on the ground between them, two offside lines are recognized. Each imaginary line runs through the back foot of the hindmost player on each team, parallel to the goal line. Players may not join a ruck from an offside position. Even onside players must enter the ruck from behind the last player's foot, not from the side. Players not participating in the ruck must move behind the offside line.

During a maul, when the ballcarrier is held by one or more opponents and one or more of the ball carrier's teammates binds onto him, two offside lines are recognized. As during a ruck, the lines run parallel to each team's goal line. To remain onside, players must join the maul from behind or alongside the hindmost foot of the hindmost player.

Coming to Terms

Age-grade rugby: Rugby played by players ages 6 to 18.

Ankle tap: A last-resort move in which the defender taps the ballcarrier on the ankle from behind in an attempt to stop him and bring him down.

Attack: The activity of the team in possession of the ball as they try to score.

Back five: The five players who, along with the scrumhalf and flyhalf, are known as backs.

Back row: The two flankers and the number 8, whose job is to stop the opposition's attacks and create attack opportunities for their team.

Backs (or three-quarters): The generally faster athletes who play outside the scrummage and line-out.

Back three: Players who defend against kicks, initiate counterattacks, and act as strike runners in support of the mid-field attack.

Ballcarrier: The player carrying the ball.

Bind: To firmly grasp another player's body from the shoulder to the hips with the whole arm, from hand to shoulder, normally during scrums, rucks, mauls, and line-outs.

Blind side: The area of the field between the ball and the closest touchline.

Box kick: A punt, normally by a scrumhalf or flyhalf, that flies over and beyond a scrummage or line-out for teammates to chase.

Breakdown: When play transitions from one phase to another, usually after a tackle and the subsequent struggle for possession.

Center: The player who clears the way for the winger.

Chip kick: A kick that sails just over and behind a pursuing opponent, intended for the kicker herself or a teammate to catch.

Continuity: Maintaining possession through several consecutive phases of play.

Conversion: A kick at goal after a try is scored.

Dead ball: A stoppage in play.

Defense: The activity of the team not in possession of the ball, who attempt to prevent the opposing team from scoring.

Drift defense: A type of defense played by backs, in which they gradually shift from the players immediately opposite them to tackle players farther away.

Used primarily when the attackers pass the ball too early or when they run at an angle toward the touchline.

Drive: When players (usually forwards) bind together into a close group and push opponents back toward their own goal line.

Drop goal: A drop kick that sails over the crossbar, between the goalposts, to score 3 points.

Drop kick: A kick in which the player drops the ball, point first, and boots it as it makes contact with the ground.

Field of play (playing area): The area between but not including the goal lines and touchlines.

Flanker: The player who serves as a link between the backs and the forwards in attack and on defense.

Flyhalf: The player who receives from the forwards after they receive from the scrumhalf. Known as the primary on-field decision maker and tactician.

Forwards: The players who participate in scrums and line-outs.

Front five: Players positioned in the front row and the middle two positions of the second row in the scrum.

Front row: Players who make direct contact with the opposing team during the scrum.

Fullback: The "last line of defense" player who penetrates during the attack.

Gain line: The imaginary line between opposing teams that marks the place the attacking players would need to reach in order for the ball to be ahead of the forwards.

Grubber kick: A kick deliberately sent rolling on the ground.

Gut pass: A close-contact pass in which the ball does not leave the passer's hands until it is pushed up and delivered into the receiver's midriff.

Halfbacks: The scrumhalf and flyhalf.

Hooker: The player whose duties include throwing the ball into the line-out and hooking the ball back in the scrum.

In-goal: The area between the goal line and the dead-ball line and between the touch-in goal lines. The goal line itself is included in this area, but the others are not.

Inside center: The center playing next to the flyhalf.

Kick: Striking the ball with any part of the foot (except the heel) or any part of the leg from toe to knee.

Kickoff: The play used to start the game (at the beginning or after halftime) in which one team kicks the ball from the center of the halfway line toward the opposing team.

Knock-on (throw forward): When a player loses possession of the ball and it goes forward. Also, when a player hits the ball forward with his hand or arm so that the ball touches the ground or another player before the first player can catch it again.

Line of touch: The imaginary line at right angles to the touchline where the ball is thrown in from touch.

Line-out: The method of restarting play after the ball goes into touch (out of bounds) in which the forwards from each team line up in rows facing each other, forming a tunnel between them, and the team with possession of the ball throws it in. Note: The ball must go straight down the middle of the tunnel.

Locks (or second row): The two forwards, often the tallest players on the team, who jump for the ball in the line-out and during kickoffs. The locks also provide strength in the scrum, forming the second row or the "engine room."

Loitering: When a player stands or retreats into an offside position.

Loop: When a player runs around a teammate to whom he has just passed the ball, intending to receive the ball back from him. A "loop pass" is a pass made in this situation.

Loosie: A name for the three players who make up the back row, so called because they are supposed to be the first to reach a loose ball.

Loose-head prop: The player on the left hand side of the scrum (closest to the scrumhalf) who also supports the jumper in the jump-and-catch sequence in the line-out.

Maul: A formation in which the ballcarrier is being held by one or more opponents and one or more of the ballcarrier's teammates binds onto him. All players involved are on their feet and moving toward a goal line, while open play has stopped.

Middle five: The halfbacks and back-row forwards.

Mid-field: Refers to the middle of the playing field as well as the players (the flyhalf and two centers) working that area.

No side: The end of the match.

Number 8: The player who typically packs down in the third row of the scrum and often serves as the extra jumper at the rear of the line-out.

Open side: The area between the ball and the farthest touchline.

Openside flanker: The flanker who binds on the open side of the scrum.

Out of play: When the ball goes into touch or touch-in-goal, or when the ball touches or crosses the dead-ball line.

Outside center: The back who plays next to the winger on either side of the field.

Overlap: When a team has more players in an attacking line than the opposition.

Pack: The entire group of forwards.

Peel: When a forward runs around the front or back of the line-out to move the ball upfield from a catch or tap.

Pick and go: A forward charge in which the ball is placed on the ground at the tackle and another forward quickly picks it up and resumes the attack.

Pitch: The playing field.

Place kick: Kicking the ball from where it has been placed on the ground.

Props: The two forwards (loose-head and tight-head) who support the hooker in the scrum and lift the jumpers in the line-out.

Punt: The most commonly used kick in a match. The player deliberately drops the ball and strikes it with his foot before it hits the ground.

Pushover try: When players are able to keep the ball under their feet and push the opposition scrum across the try line.

Put-in: When the scrumhalf puts the ball into the scrum.

Quick throw-in: When the ball is thrown in before the line-out forms.

Recycle: Maintaining possession and advancing the ball following contact (such as an attempted tackle) with the opposing side.

Reserve bench: Where the replacement players sit during a match.

Roll: When a player plants his foot firmly on the ground, then pivots away from the area.

Ruck: A formation in which one or more players from each team are on their feet and in contact, closing around the ball, which is on the ground between them. Once a ruck is formed, players may use only their feet (no hands) to get the ball.

Running line: The direction a player runs in either attack or defense.

Screw punt: A type of punt in which the ball spirals in the air, thus increasing the distance it travels.

Scrum (or scrummage): A formation in which eight players from each team bind in against the other team with the purpose of winning the ball, which is thrown in between the front rows of the two packs. The scrum is used to restart the game following an infringement.

Scrumhalf (or halfback): The player who puts the ball into the scrum and usually distributes it from scrums, rucks, mauls, and line-outs.

Scrum machine: An apparatus used during training for teams to practice their scrummaging skills.

Set piece: A set formation used to restart play, such as a scrum or line-out.

Sevens: An abbreviated form of rugby in which teams of seven players compete on a full field for 7 minutes per half.

Shortened line-out: When the throw-in team uses fewer than seven players in the line-out.

Strike runners: Players who run into open spaces and attempt to score.

Support: Following the ballcarrier in order to assist if he is tackled or is looking for a pass receiver.

Tackle: When a player makes contact with an opponent carrying the ball and brings him down to the ground.

Tackle line: An imaginary line designating the points where the attack and defense would meet if they ran straight toward each other.

Throw-in: When the ball is thrown into the line-out from touch.

Tight-head (or tight-head prop): Known as the anchor of the scrum, this is the player on the right side of the scrum who packs in opposite where the scrumhalf puts the ball in. He also supports the jumper in the jump-and-catch sequence in the line-out and kickoffs.

Touch: The point where the ball is out of play after it makes contact with a touchline, the ground, or a person or an object on or beyond the touchline, or when the ballcarrier makes contact with a touchline or the ground beyond it.

Touch-in-goal line: The extension of the touchline from corner flag to dead-ball line.

Touchline: The two lines that define the sides of the field, running from corner flag to corner flag.

Try: The method of scoring (worth 5 points) in which an attacking player grounds the ball in the opposition's in-goal area.

Try line (or goal line): The line at either end of the field that the ballcarrier must cross to score a try.

Up and under (also called Garryowen): Tactical kick that sails high in the air while defenders run toward the opposition waiting to make the catch.

Wheel: When a scrum turns more than 90 degrees.

Wings (or wingers): The two attacking players, usually the fastest on the team, who play closest to the touchline.

Wipers kick: A kick that sends the ball traveling diagonally across the field, crossing over and behind the opponent's defense to land behind the far winger and roll toward the corner.

Wooden spoon: Nickname given to the last-place team in a tournament.

Zone defense: A system in which defenders cover one particular area of the field and tackle any ballcarrier that enters that space.

5: Fun in the Scrum

Skills, Drills, and On-Pitch Thrills

Even though Jonah Lomu was born big and powerful, it took years of practice before he was elevated to superstar status on the All Blacks. Sure, Jason Leonard was a gifted athlete from the time he could walk, but it was hard work that made him England's top prop.

Many rugby unions worldwide encourage coaches of young players, especially those brand-new to the game, to emphasize core skills, rather than complex game plans or winning philosophies. Players need to be able to handle the ball, kick the ball, and pass and catch effectively from both sides before coaches can introduce team runs and back plays. Before a player even thinks of attempting a famous move such as the All Black Runaround, she needs to get her head around the basics. Then she can begin to master the finer points of the game.

Hands On

Every position player, from scrumhalf to halfback, needs to learn good ball-handling skills. Before you can successfully kick, pass, or run with the ball, it stands to reason that you need to have control of it.

Step one: a good grip.

Hold It Right There

Here are a few tips to help you get a grip:

- Whenever possible, hold the ball with two hands.
- Grasp the ball firmly, with your fingers spread across the seams.
- Use the seams to maintain your grip.
- Use your fingers, not your palms, to control the ball.

When you're running downfield, a great way to maintain control and keep the ball away from defenders is to hold the ball along your forearm or to tuck it into your ribs in the crook of your elbow. This way, you can pump your arms while running as fast as you can and still protect the ball. Remember, when you cradle the ball in this fashion, you'll need to return to a two-handed grip before you attempt a pass.

It's also important to learn to control the ball in contact situations, especially

Be sure to tuck it in.

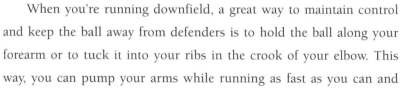

tackles. Try to maintain possession during the tackle by carrying the ball in the arm farthest away from the defender. That way, you can use your other arm to fend off the opponent or even to push off of him when he moves in to try to tackle you. If you do make contact, be sure to keep your body between the ball and the defender.

TIP FOR PLAYERS

Players with strong fingers are more likely to keep their hold on the ball. Some coaches recommend squeezing tennis balls or carrying around heavy bricks to build finger strength.

PASSING

In rugby, the runner's objective is to move the ball as far downfield as possible, passing the ball to a teammate before defenders move in for a tackle. The main thing to remember is that you're not allowed to pass forward, only backward (away from your try line) or horizontally (parallel to the try line).

Lateral or Backward Pass

How?

Hold the ball upright in both hands, with one hand on either side of the ball, fingers spread wide. Swing the ball across your body in the direction away from the target. (If the pass is intended to go right, swing the ball to the left side of your body.) Then swing your arms and shoulders toward the intended receiver and let go of the ball. Be sure to toss the ball hard, high, and fast enough so it reaches its target.

When?

Pass only when the intended receiver is in a better position than you are to continue moving downfield. Don't pass to a teammate surrounded by defenders who may tackle him or intercept the ball.

Where?

When defenders close in, pass!

Pass the ball slightly in front of the intended receiver so he can catch it on the run. Aim your throw so he can catch the ball between his waist and chest. Be sure to follow through with your arms after the pass so your fingers point to your target.

Gut Pass

When the ballcarrier is closely guarded by a defender but still has a teammate nearby, the best option may be a gut pass, which resembles a football hand-off.

What?

A pass that is basically handed from the ballcarrier to his teammate, rather than thrown.

When?

The ballcarrier is under pressure and gives the ball to a teammate with better position.

How?

- Turn away from the defender, either by bumping into his lower chest (leading with your lowered shoulder and turning away) or swerving and pivoting away from him.

- Push the ball away from yourself as you turn, keeping it visible to your closest teammate.

- Pass or hand the ball into your teammate's hands. Your teammate collects the ball by placing one hand on top and one hand underneath.

- Support the new ballcarrier immediately.

TIP FOR PLAYERS

Learn to pass with both your right and left hands. This is especially important for the scrumhalf, who passes from the scrum. (The majority of passes made from the base of the scrum come from the left side.)

PASSES FOR DUMMIES

Every time a player contemplates a pass to a teammate, he has another option: the dummy pass. This fake pass works well when the ballcarrier spots a defender moving toward his intended target.

Basically, a dummy pass is made the same way as an actual pass, only the ballcarrier keeps his fingers wrapped around the ball instead of releasing it, then quickly pulls the ball back in toward his body.

Dummies are very effective, but beware: Fake it too often and the opposition will be on to you.

CATCHING

Catching the ball seems like a straightforward skill. But since balls sail toward players from all directions in various scenarios, all catches are not created equal.

When preparing to receive the ball from a pass, you will most likely be running and on the attack. Since passes can be made only backward or laterally, you will be facing forward (toward your team's try line) or angled slightly in the direction of the passer.

First, make a target for the passer by holding your hands out toward him at chest height with both palms facing the ball. After he throws the ball to you, collect it with your fingertips, not your palms. Be sure to watch the ball all the way into your hands. Then readjust the ball in your hands before running or passing.

Make a target with your hands.

When catching the ball from a kick (which approaches from behind), you should turn sideways in the direction of the oncoming ball, even when you are running. This will help you to control the ball and prevent you from dropping it forward, which would result in a turnover. Also, the sideways stance allows you to use your shoulders to protect yourself from any would-be tacklers.

"Three times a week I try to visualize different aspects of my game that need improving. I also set myself regular short-term goals to focus on during training and matches."—KELLY MCCALLUM, FLYHALF, CANADIAN WOMEN'S NATIONAL TEAM

What's the Point?

Note: When the ball is in the air and you are moving into position for the catch, it helps to call to your teammates, "My ball!"

To ensure a successful catch:

- Stay balanced and try to keep your feet at least shoulder distance apart.
- As the ball approaches, raise your arms, spread your fingers, and turn your palms upwards, keeping them soft.
- Catch the ball in your spread fingers and pull the ball down to your chest and arms.
- As you pull the ball in, lower into a slightly crouched position and face sideways, away from your opponent.

Tip for Players

Always strive for a two-handed catch, but remember, when a ball is coming toward you from the right, you may need to use your left hand to stop it, then both hands to control it. When the ball approaches from the left, use your right hand to stop it, then readjust to hold the ball so you are holding it with both hands.

"Tackling is 90 percent courage." —FORT LAUDERDALE COACH BILL SHELLEY

ALL THE RIGHT MOVES

Stop it with one.
Catch it with two.

When rugby players are in contact on the field, it's often difficult, especially for spectators, to tell exactly what's going on. Though it may look like chaos from the sidelines, that struggling cluster of bodies is actually one of several distinct plays—a tackle, a ruck, or a maul—each with its own purpose and rules.

The tackle begins with two or more players on their feet, one of whom must be the ballcarrier, and ends when the ballcarrier is brought to the ground and/or the ball touches the ground while the ballcarrier is being held. Following the tackle, the ballcarrier must immediately pass the ball to a teammate or release it by placing it on the ground (ideally in a position where a teammate can scoop it up). The tackled player must immediately roll away from the ball and may not rejoin play until he is back on his feet. The same goes for the tackler.

When the ball is contested by two or more players immediately following a tackle, the play almost always turns into one of two formations—either a ruck or a maul. You will see literally dozens of rucks and mauls over the course of every match. Although the actual scenarios are much more involved, there's a simple way for spectators to tell the difference between the two: During a ruck, the ball is on the ground. During a maul, the ball is off the ground.

TACKLING

Most young American athletes learn to tackle football-style, literally using their helmet-covered heads or other padded body parts to knock runners to the ground. In rugby, tackling is an entirely different animal. "In football, you were taught to put your face in the chest of the ballcarrier—hit him in the numbers!" says Cal Rugby trainer and coach Tom Billups. "This would be catastrophic in rugby. The tackler's head should be up and behind the ballcarrier's body."

On the rugby pitch, no blocking is allowed and defenders may tackle only the attacker who is carrying the ball. Unlike in American football, rugby players don't tackle each other just to stop the play. Mostly, they tackle each other to win possession of the ball.

According to Coach Tom Billups, every tackle consists of five sequential phases:

The Close: Don't sit and wait. Close in on the attacker.

The Set-Up: Get stable. Position yourself so your last step corresponds with the shoulder you will use to tackle. (For example, to tackle with your right shoulder, step on your right foot.)

The Strike: With your head up and behind the ballcarrier, strike with the shoulder and step with the foot on the same side.

The Wrap: Wrap your arms (leading with the arm on the same side as the strike) around the ballcarrier's waist.

BARING IT ALL

Every American rugby player has heard the comment, "What? You guys don't wear pads?" Although some players wear limited padding, including thin, soft headgear, what surprises rugby neophytes is the sight of players tackling each other with virtually no protection. Advocates of the game point out that rugby players might actually be more careful than football players (especially of their heads and necks), for the very reason that they are not wearing helmets and heavy pads. Any rugby player who hits an opponent with his head immediately learns that this is a very bad thing to do. Plus, unlike football players, rugby players can't use their helmets as weapons and risk injuring other players.

In rugby, safe and effective tackling is more about leverage and angles than pure power. From the first day on the pitch, coaches should teach players to tackle in a safe manner by engaging with the shoulder, then wrapping with the arms, to bring opponents down to the ground.

Engage, then wrap!

The Finish: Keep your feet moving (don't stop) to continue driving the ballcarrier back toward his own try line.

Although some elements remain constant—for example, always keep your eyes open and look at the target!—tacklers will need to vary their technique according to the position of the attacker. Tackles are made from the front, side, or behind.

Side Tackle (Side-On Tackle)

- Place your head behind the attacker's legs, and brace your shoulders.
- Keep your head up, your chin off your chest, and your neck stable.
- Use your shoulder to strike the attacker's thigh.

- Drive with your legs, wrap your arms around the ballcarrier's legs, and grip with your arms and hands.

Rear Tackle (Tackle-from-Behind)

- Place your head to one side of the ballcarrier's legs, and brace your shoulders.
- Keep your head up, your chin off your chest, and your neck stable.
- Drive with your legs, and strike the ballcarrier's buttocks with the shoulder.
- Wrap your arms around the ballcarrier's legs, and grip with your arms and hands.
- Aim to land on top of the ballcarrier.

Front Tackle (Driving Tackle)

- Drop into a crouch to receive the impact of the ballcarrier on one shoulder.
- Keep the head up (to one side of the ballcarrier's body), your chin off your chest, and your neck stable.
- Wrap your arms around the ballcarrier's legs, and grip tightly with your arms and hands.
- Allow the momentum to take the ballcarrier over your shoulder.

TIP FOR PLAYERS

During contact of any kind—tackles, rucks, mauls, and scrums—an important rule to remember is "Shoulders always above hips."

- Twist to land on top of the tackled player's legs (to the right if you're using your right shoulder, to the left if using the left shoulder).

DO:

- Tackle with confidence.
- Aim to hit your opponent between the hips and knees.
- Launch your tackle from a low, balanced position.
- Wrap with your arms.
- Avoid flying knees and elbows by placing your head to the ballcarrier's side.
- Release the ballcarrier once he is down.
- Try to gain possession of the ball.

DON'T:

- Be tentative. You're more likely to get injured if you don't tackle with full effort.
- Strike your opponent above his shoulder line.
- Use your head as a weapon.
- Trip the attacker.
- Smash into your opponent. Instead, strive to artfully take him to the ground.

As players advance, they will add more specific types of tackles to their rugby regimen, including the ball-and-all tackle, in which the player prevents the ballcarrier from passing; the stationary tackle, which resembles the ball-and-all tackle, except the player remains stationary while the ballcarrier runs right toward her; or the ankle-tap, in which she brings the ballcarrier down by hitting his feet with her hand.

Rucks and Mauls

During the transition period (called "the breakdown") that follows every tackle, both teams have an opportunity to gain possession of the ball, which, besides scoring, is the main objective of the game. Sometimes things go smoothly, and the tackled player is able to pass or release the ball to a teammate who takes off and runs with it. But more often than not, there is pressure from defenders, and the breakdown immediately evolves into a battle for the ball. Depending on the location of the ball, players will almost always form a ruck (if the ball is released on the ground) or a maul (if the ball is in a player's hands).

Ground Control

Every player who handles the ball will be tackled, so it's important to learn how to make contact with the ground. In other words, you need to practice how to fall down safely.

■ Go with the impact and roll naturally.

■ Round your shoulders and try to hit the ground as softly as possible.

■ Don't use your arms to break your fall or hit the ground with your limbs extended.

■ Make sure the ball is the last thing to hit the ground.

The ruck stops here.

The Ruck

What?

The formation in which two or more players, at least one from each team, are on their feet and in physical contact, closing around the ball on the ground between them.

When?

To obtain the ball from the ground, after a teammate has been tackled in open play. Most often formed when play is moving forward.

How to Set Up the Ruck from the Breakdown

Ballcarrier

- Attempt to bump your tackler away with your leading shoulder.
- If you are being held, turn toward your support players.
- Slowly go to the ground.
- Place the ball at arm's length behind you, toward your support players.
- Place your hands over your ears, elbows up, to protect your head.
- Roll away from the ruck, and, as quickly as possible, get back on your feet.

Support Players

- With your eyes open, head forward, back flat, and shoulders above your hips, drive forward over the tackled player.
- Shrug your shoulders, and loosen your neck as you make contact.
- Bind onto another player, either a teammate or an opponent.
- Drive forward and low with your body, keeping your eyes open, head forward, back flat, and shoulders above your hips.
- Stay on your feet, and attempt to keep your opponents on their feet.

Opposition Players

While attacking players form the ruck, opposing players may join in at any time and attempt to stop their progress. Opposition players

enter the ruck in the same fashion as attacking players, by binding onto another player, either a teammate or an opponent. The most important thing is to enter the ruck safely, making sure that your head and shoulders are no lower than your hips when your make contact.

Probably the most challenging part of a ruck, especially for new players, is how to get in position.

First, bind onto another player.

As we discussed in Chapter 4, players should strive to remain onside at all times before, during, and after the ruck. The main thing to remember is not to enter the formation from the side, but rather, from behind the last player's foot. Also, players should take care not to loiter at the ruck, which means that if you're not participating in the play, you need to move behind the offside line (behind the hindmost foot of the last player).

Regarding actual positioning of your body during the ruck, the *Laws of the Game* states that:

> All players forming, joining, or taking part in a ruck must have their
> heads and shoulders no lower than their hips. A player joining a
> ruck must bind onto the ruck with at least one arm around the body

of a teammate, using the whole arm. Placing a hand on another player in the ruck does not constitute binding. All players forming, joining, or taking part in a ruck must be on their feet.

The goal of the ruck is for your team to emerge with the ball. The challenge here is that you are not allowed to use your hands. You may only use your feet to rake the ball back toward a teammate. Since referees watch closely for unsafe play in the ruck, players should avoid making deliberate contact with an opponent who is on the ground unless part of his body is blocking access to the ball. (Exception: the player's head. Never step on or make contact with anyone's head). Kicking an opponent, especially one who has fallen, will result in an immediate penalty or often, expulsion from the game.

The ruck is complete when one team wins the ball and hands it to the halfback at the back of the formation, who distributes it to the waiting scrumhalf. At any point, if the ruck collapses or becomes unplayable, the referee will stop everything and immediately call a scrum. Otherwise, it's play on!

TIES THAT BIND

In rugby, there are several scenarios where players "bind" onto each other, which means that one player grasps another player's body from the shoulder to the hips with his entire arm, from hand to shoulder.

During a ruck, players bind onto the nearest player and close in around the ball, which is on the ground, and try to foot it backward. During a maul, the ballcarrier's teammates bind onto him, the tighter the better, to protect him from defenders looking to steal the ball away.

During the scrum, which is a formation used to restart play, the rules for binding are more specific. For example, the *Laws* states that hookers may bind over or under the arms of their props, around their bodies at or below armpit level. Although coaches should never over-choreograph binding for the scrum, teams should definitely practice which player binds onto who and when.

During the ruck, support players should do their best to arrive at the point of contact before the defensive players and gain an edge by immediately beginning the drive forward.

The Maul

What?

The formation in which two or more players, at least one from each team, are on their feet and in physical contact with the player who has possession of the ball.

When?

Formed when your team is retreating and needs time to recover control of the ball. Open play has ended, and all players are on their feet and moving toward a goal line.

How to Set Up the Maul from the Breakdown
Ballcarrier

- With your eyes open and head up, make a long, low stride toward your defender.
- With your body weight over your front foot, tuck your chin toward your chest, and step to the defender's side.
- While holding the ball firmly against your chest with both

If you stay on your feet, the opposition will retreat.

hands, shrug your shoulders, turn sideways slightly, and drive up into the defender's midriff with the point of your front shoulder.

- Bend your knees, and stay on your feet as you look ahead and continue driving with your legs.
- Keep the ball visible to your support players if possible, or call out to let them know you have the ball.

Support Players

- With your eyes on the ball, drive up and under the ball while keeping your shoulders parallel to the goal lines.
- Grab the ballcarrier between the waist and shoulders, and use your shoulder to create a barrier and protect him (and the ball) from the opposition.

Note: Once a supporting player has entered the maul (as above), she may do one of several things: take the ball from the ballcarrier and run with it, take and pass the ball, hold onto the ball with the ballcarrier until a teammate becomes available to take the ball, or prevent the opposition from getting the ball. All supporting players should contribute to the maul by driving it forward, protecting the ball, and keeping everyone on their feet.

Opposition Players

While attacking players form the maul, opposing players may join in at any time and attempt to stop their progress. Opposition players enter the maul in the same fashion as attacking players, by binding on to another player, either a teammate or an opponent. It is very difficult to stop a maul, but defenders may succeed in slowing its forward progress by making contact with the front players with full force, making sure to connect at an angle lower than the opposite player.

According to the *Laws of the Game*, here's how to play it safe in the maul:

Players joining a maul must have their heads and shoulders no lower than their hips. A player must be caught in or bound to the maul and not just alongside it. Placing a hand on another player in the maul does not constitute binding. Players in a maul must endeavor to stay on their feet. The ballcarrier in a maul may go to ground providing the ball is available immediately and play continues. A player must not intentionally collapse a maul or jump on top of a maul.

TIP FOR PLAYERS

Try your best to keep the maul moving. A static maul, where too many players have their hands on the ball, is not very effective! That said, a slow, steady speed with all players in sync works better than a full-speed, uncoordinated approach.

Much like rucks, mauls can be used by the attacking team as a ploy to disorganize the defense. A team often forms a maul directly following a line-out, since players are clustered together in one area and can get in position quickly. At other times, a maul is created when the ballcarrier makes contact with a tackler (who puts his hands on the ball) and turns away, seeking the help of his teammates to wrest back control of the ball. Mauls may be further classified into driving mauls, where the attacking team attempts to drive through the opposition, and rolling mauls, where the attacking team's players transfer the ball to a teammate on the side of the maul which has the least number of defenders, then "roll" or continually move around to that side as they progress downfield.

Communication is key during mauls. Not only do players talk to each other inside the formation, they are further directed by the scrumhalf, who stands nearby calling out instructions while waiting to receive the ball.

As we noted in Chapter 4 and in the discussion of rucking above, players must strive to remain onside at all times, especially when entering and leaving the maul. And, as always, safety must be the first priority. Never attempt to pull an opponent out of a maul (even if he is offside), and never jump on a maul or attempt to collapse it, or you will be called for dangerous play.

A maul ends successfully when the ball or the ballcarrier leaves the maul or the ball goes to ground or the player holding the ball touches or crosses over the goal line. A maul ends unsuccessfully if it stops moving for more than 5 seconds, if the ball becomes unplayable, or if the maul collapses. When the maul doesn't work, the ref calls for a scrum.

SET PIECES

When play has stopped for any reason, it is restarted in certain situations by a kick (see "Starts and Restarts" on page 86). If a kick is not called for, the match will restart with one of two possible formations, the scrum and the line-out, which are known as set pieces.

Note: Many youth leagues do not allow scrums and line-outs, especially for players age ten and younger. If they do, they often impose restrictions, such as limiting the length of the drive during the scrum

or forbidding jumping during line-outs. Consult http://www.usarugby.
org or your local league's rules to be sure.

THE SCRUM

When people think of rugby, they think of the scrum. This signature
formation, in which eight players from each team connect, push against
each other, and scramble with their feet for the ball, is unique to this
sport. And nothing irks a rugby player more than when someone unfamiliar with the game disparages the scrum. Even though it looks to the
untrained eye like a disorganized tangle of arms and legs, the scrum
(or scrummage) is actually a technically precise undertaking and a key
element of the game.

Scrums are used to restart play after the referee calls a minor
infringement or after the game has been stopped for one of several
other reasons, such as a collapsed maul. To form a scrum, eight forwards from each team bind together against each other and compete for
the ball, which is thrown in between the front rows of the two packs.

**Crouch! Touch!
Pause! Engage!**

The scrum comprises several components: binding, positioning, engaging, putting-in, and winning the ball. Keep in mind that finesse is more important than sheer force, so the focus should always be on technique and proper form.

The Pack

Eight players from each team participate in the scrum. They are:

- Front row: the hooker and the two props
- Second row: the two locks
- Back row: the two flankers and the number 8

The hooker is so named because he hooks the ball with his foot and channels it back to his teammates during the scrum. The props got their name from their job, which is to prop up the hooker. The loose-head prop plays on the left-hand side of the scrum, the tight-head prop plays on the right. The locks and flankers also got their names from their function and positioning in the scrum. And the number 8? Since he plays so many roles, he has no nickname, unless you want to call him the leader of the pack.

Note: Because safety is so important in a complicated maneuver such as the scrum, the *Laws* dictates that only experienced players may play in or be substituted into the front row.

Binding

The *Laws of the Game* is very specific about the proper way for players to bind in the scrum. (These specifications keep evolving, so be sure to read the most current edition of the *Laws*!) First, the hooker—the anchor of the scrum—takes his place and raises his arms so the two props can bind onto him by sliding a shoulder under one of his arms and sliding one arm firmly around his waist. Once the hooker is solidly linked with the props, these three players—now forming the front row—adjust their body positioning and prepare for pressure from the second row by bending their knees, lowering their hips, and leaning back slightly.

Next, the second row moves into position, with the two locks placing their inside arms around each other's waists, bending forward, then placing one shoulder against the back of one of the hooker's upper thighs and the other shoulder on one of the prop's upper thighs. Lastly, each lock puts his spare arm through one of the prop's legs (the one closest to him) and grabs his waistband in the front from below. Once in position, the locks' heads should poke out between the props' and the hooker's hips.

Finally, the back row binds onto the second row. First, each flanker stands behind one of the locks, reaches across his back, and grasps him tightly. Then the number 8 slots in at the back of the scrum, pushing his shoulders against the two locks' backsides, binding his arms around the outside of their hips, and placing his head between their bodies.

Body Positioning

Once the players from each team are bound together, they are ready to engage their opponents, who are facing them in an identical formation and standing not more than an arm's length away.

At this stage, body positioning for every player is extremely important, both for safety and for effectiveness. According to *The RFU Handbook of Safe Rugby*, the basic body position of players during the scrum is characterized by:

- *Head up, chin off chest, eyes open*
- *Back flat, shoulders above hips*
- *Feet back, legs slightly bent*
- *As many studs (on shoes) in contact with the ground as possible*

As players improve, the coach may fine-tune their positioning. For example, when looking at the front row players head-on, the coach should see each player in a wide stance with his shoulders level.

Crouch! Touch! Pause! Engage!

During a match, once the scrum is in place, the referee shouts out directions: At "Crouch!" the front-row players dip down so their shoulders are just above hip level. At "Touch!" each prop touches the shoulder of the opponent opposite him. At "Pause," players are at the ready, and when the ref shouts "Engage!" the whole formation drives forward and the front-row players close up with their opponents so their heads are interlocked.

Put-In

Prior to putting the ball in, the scrumhalf stands 1 meter (1.1 yd) from the endpoint of the imaginary middle line that separates the players lined up on their respective sides of the scrum. Then he quickly throws the ball in straight along the middle line (down the tunnel) so that the

Back in 1871, a fullback who played for England in the first international match in history (against Scotland) described scrums as "long, drawn-out shoving matches, with players joining on in twos, giving the appearance of a caterpillar whose last meal had stuck halfway down."

ball touches the ground immediately beyond the width of the nearest prop's shoulders. The ball must be thrown in with a single forward movement, with no spin. Faking a throw is not allowed.

Note: Following an infringement, the fouled team puts in the ball. Following a collapsed ruck or maul, the team that did not cause the ruck or maul to collapse puts in. If it's too close to identify the nonoffending team, or in the case of a stopped ruck or maul, the team that previously had possession puts in. The scrum begins when the ball leaves the scrumhalf's hands.

Winning the Ball

After the ball touches the ground in the tunnel, any front-row player (usually the hooker) may use either of his feet to hook (win possession of) the ball. Front rowers learn the most effective approach of hooking the ball through practice; most often, a quick strike and a soft touch work best. The player who hooks the ball channels it backward between the two second rowers toward the number 8, who holds it with his feet until he is ready to play it or pass to the scrumhalf, who will then run with it or pass to a waiting back.

A scrum is complete when the ball leaves the formation from any position, excluding the tunnel. At that point, the side that won the ball may launch their attack.

Feet, do your stuff.

Note: The best attacking position is a mid-field scrum. With space on all sides, the defenders are forced to split their backs (since they don't know from which direction the attack will come). This gives the attacking team a definite advantage.

The scrumhalf plays the ball from the scrum.

Last Word

Players should consult the *Laws* to become familiar with all the particulars pertaining to the scrum. There are literally dozens of dos, from the length of time players are required to stay bound together (until the scrum is over) to where and when scrums take place (following a line-out, as a result of an infringement, and so on) and what to do when one collapses (usually, re-form and do another one). There are just as many don'ts: no falling, kneeling, driving in and up, or doing anything to collapse the scrum. The *Laws* also outlines the procedure for scrummage when a team has fewer than eight players available or five players qualified to play in the front two rows, which is especially important for safety reasons. (Players not only need to be strong to withstand the pressure of the front row, but they need to be experienced in exactly how to get into position so they don't get hurt.)

THE LINE-OUT

The most common mode of restarting play in rugby is the line-out. After the ball or the ballcarrier crosses one of the touchlines (and is called out of bounds), players from both sides line up to compete for possession of the ball, which is thrown in by the hooker from the team that did not put the ball out of bounds (or, if play was halted by a penalty, the team that did not commit the offense). The distinguishing feature of this formation is the jumper, a player hoisted high in the air by his teammates to go after the ball.

Note: Instead of waiting for a line-out to form, a team may also take a quick throw-in, in which the hooker simply steps to the touchline and throws the ball in to a nearby teammate. But beware! Quick throw-ins only work if your players are ready and the defenders are not. Only use them if you truly have the element of surprise on your side.

Tunnel vision: practicing the line-out.

What?

The two sets of forwards form two single, parallel columns at right angles to the touchline, then compete for possession after the team with the ball throws it in.

IN AND OUT OF TOUCH

During a match, when the ball goes into touch (out of bounds), the touch judge raises his flag and calls for a line-out at the point where the ball exited the field (if the ball bounced, rolled, or was carried, thrown, or driven out) or the point where the kick was made (if the ball was kicked out without touching the ground or another player).

The *Laws* gets even more specific depending on the situation (Did the ball touch the ground? Did it touch another player on its way out?) and the location (Did the kick originate behind or in front of the player's 22-meter line?).

When?

To restart play after certain penalties or when a ball goes into touch.

Where?

The ball is thrown in from behind the touchline at the point where the ball went into touch or even with the point where the ball was kicked from before it went into touch. The line-out takes place in a 10-meter-long (10.9 yd) area, from 5 meters (5.5 yd) from the touchline to a 15-meter dash line.

Who?

The standard line-out is made up of seven players per side, plus one player throwing in the ball. Besides the players in the line-out, including the all-important jumper, who catches the ball, each team also designates a receiver, who stands behind his line of players and takes the toss from the jumper. Also, the defense may designate a player, who stands between the touchline and the 5-meter line, to mark or cover the thrower.

Throwing In

The throw-in must go straight down the middle of the tunnel formed by the two rows.

How?

- Stand by the touchline, and hold the ball (pointing downward) with two hands across the seam near the back point.
- Place one foot forward, and raise the ball behind your head.

LINE 'EM UP

According to the *Laws of the Game,* a line-out is formed by at least two players from each side. The team throwing in the ball decides the actual number of players per team in the line-out. Typically, that number is seven, but some teams use more (a long line-out) or fewer (a short line-out) for strategic reasons. The opposing team may decide to use fewer players than the team with possession, but they may not use more.

- Move both hands forward to throw, keeping your hands on the ball as long as possible.
- As your body weight moves forward, release the ball, aiming for the highest point of your teammate's jump, and step onto the field.
- Immediately move into position to support the new ballcarrier.

TIP FOR PLAYERS

Hookers need to practice throwing as often as possible, not just during line-out practice. Try throwing against a wall from different distances to improve your accuracy.

Receiving

Once the throw is made, players immediately move into position to catch the ball. One player from each side jumps for it, with a little help from two supporting teammates. For obvious reasons, the jumper is usually the tallest player on the team, although many teams use different players in this role at different times.

Until 2008, the *Laws of the Game* stated: *a lineout player must not lift a teammate.* Although this law was strictly enforced in many youth leagues, for players high-school age and older, it was a gray area. Technically, players were allowed to "support" a teammate jumping in the line-out, but since it is very difficult to tell the difference between "supporting" and "lifting," few referees called penalties here unless players were doing something blatantly unfair or unsafe.

As of the 2008–09 season, though, lifting became legal as part of the introduction of the *Experimental Law Variations* (ELVs). The *Laws* now reads that *line-out players may grip a jumper before the ball is thrown in* and *the lifting of line-out jumpers is permitted*. Regardless of the ever-evolving laws or the inevitable gray areas in rugby, a player's best bet is to always play it safe.

Jump, catch!

Jumping

Listen for the signal from a designated teammate regarding whether you will be the receiver for the throw (the jumper). Be ready to fake a jump even if you are not the intended receiver.

How?

- Position yourself in a wide, steady stance, with your hands in front of you, palms facing the thrower.
- When the ball is thrown in, jump up and slightly toward the line of touch.
- Keep your eyes on the ball at all times.
- Catch the ball with both hands, bend your knees, and pull the ball toward your chest.
- Turn your back toward the opposing line.
- Release the ball to supporting teammates.

Note: If the jumper is unable to catch the ball, or if the direction of the throw presents an opportunity, he may tap the ball or gently push it with one or both hands directly to the scrumhalf.

TIP FOR THE JUMPER

Try to jump like a ballet dancer, with your toes pointed down, to keep your legs straight. The height of your jump is important, but it's more crucial to catch the ball quickly, no matter how high you jump. This way you'll gain possession of the ball before defenders have a chance to react.

Lifting

There are two lifters in the line-out: the front lifter, who stands in front of the jumper, and the back lifter, who stands behind him. Both use a similar supporting technique, but they grip the jumper differently, and the back lifter provides most of the initial boost.

How?

- Stand close to the jumper, bend your knees, and lower yourself down toward the ground, as if you're about to sit in a chair.
- Front jumper: Using both hands, grasp the jumper's thighs just above the knees.
- Back jumper: Using both hands, grasp the jumper's thighs just beneath the buttocks.
- Using the power in your legs, not your arms or your back, support the player as he jumps.

- Extend your arms over your head, and lock your arms and legs as the jumper reaches his highest point.
- After the jumper catches the ball, guide him to the ground, and immediately step in behind him to protect him from tacklers.

Note: When supporting the jumper, be sure to grab him by his legs, not his shorts, since shorts can move around and cause you to lose your grip.

The Bottom Line

The line-out begins when the ball is thrown-in and ends when the ball is passed or run out of the area between the 5- and 15-meter lines.

As with the scrum, the *Laws* lists dozens of dos and don'ts, including exactly how to line up (for example, opposing players must keep a clear space between their inside shoulders) and what moves are allowed before, during, and after the throw-in. Always consult the latest version of the *Laws* to be up-to-date in the line-out.

The most important thing is for players, especially jumpers, to protect themselves in all situations. *The RFU Handbook of Safe Rugby* points out the following safety factors in the line-out:

- *Players must not interfere with opponents who are trying to win the ball.*
- *It is better for support players to play with their heads up, looking for the ball, rather than to crouch down with their hands on their knees.*

JUST FOR KICKS

In rugby, players kick the ball to start or restart play, to score points, to gain territory, to launch an attack, or to relieve defensive pressure. Players should strive to kick with purpose—that is, for strategic reasons, not just as a last resort. As coaches say, "Kick smart!" It's better to take the tackle than to kick away the territory your team has worked hard to gain.

Depending on the game situation, players kick the ball in one of two ways: either from their hands (punt, chip kick, box kick, grubber kick, and wipers kick) or from the ground (place kick and drop kick). The scrumhalf, flyhalf, and fullback are the players most often designated for kicking duty, but every rugby player will eventually be called upon to kick.

According to the *Laws of the Game, The ball may be kicked with any part of the lower leg from the knee to the foot, excluding the knee and the heel.* But to be most effective, stick with the foot!

TIP FOR PLAYERS

"Visualize in your head exactly where you want the ball to go."

—*England's fly-half and star kicker Jonny Wilkinson*

KICKING FROM YOUR HANDS

When you hold the ball, then drop it toward your foot to kick it as it falls, you are said to be "kicking from your hands." Mostly, this kind of kicking is used for punts. A rugby punt resembles a football punt, although in rugby there are several variations, each for use in different situations.

TIP FOR COACHES

During kicking practice, place a group of players downfield to catch the balls. This way, your team can practice two skills at once.

Spiral Punt

What?

An all-purpose, highly accurate punt that spins off your foot to spiral through the air.

When?

You want the ball to travel a great distance in a straight line.

How?

- Hold the ball with both hands, with the side of the ball facing down, and extend your arms away from your body at waist height, angled down approximately 30 degrees.
- Aim the nonkicking foot at the target.

- Drop the ball straight down. As you do, shift your weight onto your nonkicking foot, and draw your kicking foot backward.
- Point your toe, swing your kicking foot straight through, and strike the ball with your instep, hitting the ball along its lengthwise center seam.
- Extend the arm opposite your kicking foot for balance, and follow through with your head down and your body over the ball.

Note: Adjust the path of the ball by slightly altering the angle of your foot and the point where you strike the ball. Through practice, you will learn how much force it takes to send the ball where you intend it to go.

Up and Under (Garryowen)

What?
A very high, short spiral punt with a long hang time.

When?
Your team wants to keep the ball in play. Boot the ball high in the air, giving your teammates time to reach the ball when it comes back down. (The ball goes up, you run under.)

How?
Similar to a spiral punt, except that you hold the ball so the point is facing down and your foot makes contact with the pointed end.

Chip Kick

What?

A short punt made to sail just over the top of the advancing defense.

When?

There is open space just behind the defenders, so you kick the ball over their heads for one of your teammates behind them to catch.

How?

Similar to an Up and Under, except you take the kick on the run, rather than from a standstill, and usually kick it more softly.

Grubber Kick (End over End)

What?

A short kick that travels low and fast across the ground.

When?

Defenders are moving in quickly, and you want to put the ball behind them. An effective restart kick in wet weather and, since it's short and accurate, a good kick for when you want to force a line-out.

How?

- Hold the ball upright across its seams with one hand on each side.
- Lean forward with your head and eyes over the ball.
- Point the toes of your kicking foot toward the ground.

- Keeping your knee bent slightly ahead of the ball, drop the ball, and strike it on its upper half with your shoe laces before it hits the ground.
- Follow through with a low, straight leg.

Other types of kicks made from the hands include the quick tap, basically a very short kick made directly to a teammate; the wipers kick, a diagonal, cross-field kick most often made by the flyhalf that travels behind the defense to set up the kicker's wingers; and a box kick, made by the scrumhalf to move the ball from the base of the scrum. And don't forget the dummy kick, where the player fakes a punt but passes or runs instead.

For detailed kicking scenarios and advice on when to use which kind of punt, check out http://coachingrugby.com.

KICKING FROM THE GROUND

When players kick the ball after placing it on the ground or after the ball hits the ground, they are said to be "kicking from the ground." These are important types of kicks, especially since they may result in field goals.

Drop Kick

What?

A kick in which the ball hits the ground before the player strikes it with his foot.

TIP FOR PLAYERS

When punting on the run, try to slow and steady yourself just before kicking. With defenders in hot pursuit, there may not be much time to do this. For this reason, players are wise to learn to kick with either foot so they can take any kick literally in stride.

When?

To restart play after a score, at 22-meter drop-outs (drop-kicks awarded to the defending team), or at the beginning of the half. Players also use this type of kick while the ball is in play to score a drop-goal (field goal) by kicking it over the crossbar and through the uprights for 3 points.

How?

- Hold the ball upright with both hands, fingers pointing down or forward, and extend the ball in front of you at waist height, with your elbows tucked in slightly.
- Shift your weight onto your nonkicking foot, and draw your kicking foot backward.
- Keep your head down over the ball, then drop the ball (point down) slightly in front of the kicking foot, angling it slightly toward you.
- Swing your kicking foot straight through, and strike the ball with your instep.
- Follow through by swinging your kicking foot above head height, keeping your eyes on the ball and the point on the ground where it lands and extending your arm (opposite your kicking foot) for balance.

Place Kick

What?

A kick made after the ball is placed on the ground or on a tee.

When?

The game situation calls for a conversion kick, penalty kick, or free kick.

How?

- Place the ball vertically on the kicking tee (you may place it on the ground but most players use a tee), and angle it slightly toward your target.
- Look at your target, and visualize the path of the ball.
- Walk four paces back, then take two steps to the left. (This is for right-footed kickers. Lefties, take two steps to the right.)
- Slowly approach the ball in a slight arc, always looking at the ball.
- During your final stride, push your hips forward, plant your nonkicking foot, and extend your arms for balance.
- Swing your kicking foot through, and strike the ball with the top of your foot (near where the big toe meets the instep), making contact at the end of the ball where the four seams meet.
- Drive the ball forward and up, extending your foot as you follow through with your kicking leg, pointing it toward the target.

Note: The above describes the most common, "round-the-corner" style of place kicking. With experience, many place kickers develop their own styles. No matter your style, you should adopt a routine that works for you and stick to it every time you kick.

A place kick made to a tee.

WHICH KICK?

The *Laws of the Game* dictates which type of kick players must make in certain game situations.

- **Conversion kick:** *place kick or drop kick*

- **Dropped goal:** *drop kick*

- **Penalty kick/free kick:** *punt, dropkick, or place kick*

- **Kickoff and restart:** *drop kick*

TIP FOR PLAYERS

If you want to see players performing different kinds of rugby kicks, log on to http://www.youtube.com and type in "rugby kicks." For even more visuals, type in "rugby line-out," "rugby scrum," or "rugby maul."

PUTTING TOGETHER THE PERFECT PRACTICE

Learning all the skills, moves, and formations it takes to play rugby is challenging at first. But once players master the basics, it's easy enough to patch it all together during practice drills that gradually integrate these newly learned skills. Before you know it, you'll be game ready.

WARM-UP

Every practice begins with a good 10-minute warm-up. According to Tom Billups, Cal Rugby's strength and conditioning coach, warm-ups serve two purposes: to get athletes ready to train and to continue to neurologically hardwire them with the most efficient running mechanics. In other words, simultaneously get 'em warm and reinforce good form.

Although players should warm up their entire bodies, it's important to concentrate on the muscles they'll be using in that particular practice. To that end, coaches may want to customize their team's warm-ups. Before a tackling session, have players do a contact warm-up. Before a passing drill, have players do a handling warm-up. Remember, it's important to vary the warm-up before practices and games so players don't become bored.

When players first hit the pitch, they should begin practice with some light jogging or ball-tossing, then move on to a series of dynamic movements. (Save static stretches for after the game.)

Some dynamic warm-ups include:

- **Walking lunges:** Players take a giant step forward with one foot, bend both legs at the knees, bring the back leg forward, and repeat with the opposite leg as they move down the field.

- **Knee raises:** Players jog down the field in a line, raising their knees to waist level with each step.
- **Sidestep:** Players run sideways, crossing one leg at a time in front of the other, then repeat in the other direction.

Once players are thoroughly warmed up, they may move on to drills or short games. The best of these emphasize more than one skill at a time.

BEST PRACTICE

The best practice sessions are:

- **Organized:** Coaches should make their practice plans ahead of time and be ready to go the minute players hit the field.

- **Purposeful:** Coaches should let players know what they are trying to accomplish at each practice. Is there something the team needs to improve upon from the last game?

- **Fun:** If practice isn't fun, players will lose enthusiasm for the game. Engage players with mini-competitions (as opposed to rote drills) where you keep score and something's at stake—say, the losing team puts the equipment away.

- **Flexible:** If the coach feels the team has mastered a certain skill or drill, or even if it's just not working on a particular day, move on to something else.

- **Fast-paced:** Keep players moving. Even during water breaks, have them "take it on the jog."

- **Active:** Coaches should try not to over talk. Practice is more productive when players spend the majority of practice time doing, not listening.

Making Contact

When it comes to rugby's rough-and-tumble side, coaches should adjust the practice to the player. For example, before teaching the mechanics of tackling to new or very young players, many coaches begin with simple drills or fun games to get players accustomed to contact. (An excellent source is the online coaching center at http://www.rugby.com.au, a site recommended by U.S. Women's National Team coach Kathy Flores, which lists drills and games by age.)

Once players are comfortable with contact, they can begin practicing basic tackling techniques by hitting tackle bags (large vinyl bags filled with foam), if available. When players are ready to begin practicing tackling with a partner, many coaches instruct them to start by facing off from a kneeling position. Often, this introductory tackling step is taught indoors, on a mat. Gradually, players can work up to squatting and standing, then progress to tackling each other from a walk, a jog, and a full-on run.

Here's how *The RFU Handbook of Safe Rugby* charts the progression:

- *Ballcarrier kneeling upright, tackler kneeling upright*
- *Ballcarrier standing, tackler kneeling upright*
- *Ballcarrier standing, tackler squatting*
- *Ballcarrier walking, tackler squatting*
- *Ballcarrier walking, tackler walking*
- *Ballcarrier jogging, tackler walking*
- *Ballcarrier jogging, tackler jogging*

TIP FOR COACHES

Try to pair up beginners for tackling drills by size and height. More experienced players may be paired according to ability.

Players should advance to the next level only when the coach feels they have mastered the previous step.

Formations such as the scrum should be broken down into their components, too, so players can learn to execute them safely and effectively. Beginning players should practice body positioning and binding extensively before they attempt a real scrum on the practice field. It helps to work players by row, building the scrum as they master each part. Only allow players to advance to engaging once they have mastered binding and positioning.

The ideal way to teach new players the fundamentals of scrummaging is on a scrum machine. This training device resembles a football blocking sled, with a row of pads mounted on a frame atop a sled or a wheeled platform. Players push against the pads (instead of other players) to simulate a live scrum and learn proper positioning in a controlled environment. Scrum machines may be hard to come by in developing rugby areas, but check with a nearby college or club team that might be willing to share.

DRILLS

Coaches should strive to be as creative as possible with practice drills. There are many excellent sources for drills, especially on the Internet. (Try the online coaching center at http://www.rugby.com.au.) Feel free to change or add on to drills, or even ask players to make up their own. This is bound to keep them sharp and awake during practice!

Back-to-Back and Wrestle

Purpose: To introduce contact.

Set-Up: Pairs of players sit back-to-back on the ground, locking arms at the elbow. They place their feet flat on the ground and bend their knees. Working together, they push through their feet and stand up, then lower themselves back to the ground. Once on the ground, each player works against his partner and leans to the right, trying to pin the partner's shoulder to the ground. Then they return to center and repeat on the other side.

Back-to-back contact.

Warm-up Passing Drill

Purpose: To warm up and get into playing mode.

Set-Up: Mark off a 15-yard square (approximately 12.5 square meters) using four cones, one in each corner. Have players form four lines, one at each corner, three or four players to a line, with the first players in lines 1 and 2 holding balls. As the first players from lines 1 and 3 run diagonally across the square toward each other, line 1 tosses the ball to line 3, who passes it right back. The players each head to the back of the opposite line, leaving

Ready? Pass!

the ball with the player now at the head of line 3. Lines 2 and 4 follow immediately, and the whole pattern repeats.

Variation: Move the lines clockwise around the square instead of diagonally across it, with players passing to the players behind them. Then switch to counter-clockwise.

Hot Potato Drill

Purpose: To improve ball-handling skills.

Set-Up: Players stand in a circle, each with a ball. Working solo, they pass the ball from hand to hand, passing it between their legs in a figure 8, then around their heads and shoulders.

The more touches, the better.

Tip: Think of the ball as a hot potato, getting it out of one hand and into the other as quickly as possible.

Variation: At the whistle, players pass to the left or right (on the coach's call) and repeat the exercise.

TIP FOR COACHES

Whenever possible, work players in small groups. Mark Bitcom, the trainer for Scotland's national team, groups players by position and works them three to four players at a time.

Think fast!

Swift shift.

Double Pass

Purpose: To improve hand-eye coordination and communication between teammates.

Set-Up: Players stand in a circle, every other player holding a ball. Players holding balls then take off running across the circle diagonally, passing the balls across the circle to teammates and calling out the receivers' names as they do. Soon, balls are flying and players are basically catching and passing in the same motion.

Sidestep Drill

Purpose: To improve footwork and help players learn how to swerve to beat an opponent while running with the ball.

Set-Up: Players line up one-on-one, runner vs. defender, facing each other. The runner, holding the ball in both hands, runs toward her opponent at an angle. As she approaches the defender, she plants her outside foot and shifts her weight over it. Then she quickly shifts her weight away from the planted foot and drives past the defender to the inside. Once past her, the player accelerates into open space, then returns to the end of the line.

Tips: Keep your eyes on the defender at all times. When you swerve left, hold the ball with your left hand and arm and pull it to the left side of your chest, and vice versa on the right. Fend off your defender with your free arm and hand.

Variation: Begin the drill with just the runner moving in a predetermined pattern or reacting to the coach's call ("Swerve left!") Next, add the defender. As players progress, add a second or third defender to each pairing.

Kicking Relay

Purpose: To improve punting accuracy.

Set-Up: Players form two lines, with the first player in each line holding the ball. On the whistle, players run (carrying the ball) to a marker, then turn and punt the ball to the next player in line. Each kicker runs to the back of his line as the second players run, punt, and return.

Variation: Make the drill a race between teams.

Precision kicks.

KNOW THE DRILL

- Split players into groups. Then split those groups into smaller groups so everyone is active all the time.

- Plan practice so several drills are going on at once.

- When demonstrating a skill, use several players, not just one.

- Think small. Set up drills to take place in a small space so players get moving quickly.

- Use several balls during a drill, not just one.

- Explain the purpose of the drill. Players who know what they are doing and why will be more motivated.

TIP FOR COACHES

Encourage players to stay active during the off-season or when you have a break in your regular season, but as a rule, keep it light. Some coaches call this "active rest." Players benefit from jogging, swimming, riding bikes, or playing tennis during their time off. Coaches and players will perform better in practice and on match days after a break.

6: TRAINING DAY

Getting in Shape for the Pitch

Gone are the days when rugby players (or any competitive athletes) simply showed up at the first practice of the season intending to play their way into shape. Ruggers should be in game shape from day one. Some athletes accomplish this by training on their own. Some athletes seek out other sports to play during the off-season in addition to hitting the gym. Either way, conditioning is often the secret to a successful season.

A well-conditioned athlete is a better player. Plus, a well-conditioned athlete plays it safe—players who tire easily lose concentration and risk getting hurt.

Run, Run, Run!

True, rugby players need plenty of skills. But before attempting an Aussie Loop or a Welsh Option, ruggers need to build up their endurance to keep up the pace of a nonstop game with only a short break at halftime. Players new to the game may struggle with this at first, especially football or baseball players used to getting a break after every play.

"If you love rugby, but you don't love to run, we call you a spectator," says Tom Billups, Cal Rugby's strength and conditioning coach. "Running is critical. You can have all the rugby knowledge and all the skills possible, but if you can't keep up with the pace or get to the spot on the field where you're needed, you're not going to be that helpful."

Since rugby requires short bursts of energy piled atop long periods of constant exertion, players are utilizing both their aerobic and their anaerobic systems. Usually, the anaerobic system produces the majority of the energy when a player is highly active and the aerobic system kicks in during recovery periods.

In any case, there's only one way to increase endurance (and, eventually, to increase speed): by running. And running a lot. Players should run as much as possible during practice as well as on their own time.

Run! Faster!

Since rugby players constantly change their pace, running long distances followed by short sprints, often with a change of direction, they

WHAT'S CARDIO?

Rugby players need to be able to run constantly in short bursts as well as long stretches. For this reason, athletes must be in good cardiovascular shape. "Cardio" means heart. So when you "do cardio" you are improving your heart's ability to function and pump fresh blood to your muscles as you run. You are also strengthening your respiratory system, which is why you don't get out of breath as easily when you're in shape.

Endurance athletes, such as rugby players, should aim to train in their aerobic zone, the stage of a workout where the body utilizes stored oxygen, at 70 to 80 percent of the maximum heart rate. To calculate your estimated maximum heart rate, subtract your age from 220. Then calculate 70 to 80 percent of that number to get your zone.

The following calculation is for a sixteen-year-old:

Max heart rate: 220–16 = 204

80 percent of 204   = 163

70 percent of 204   = 142

So a sixteen-year-old should aim for a heart rate between 142 and 163 beats per minute during her workout. Measure your heart rate by putting your index finger on the large artery of your wrist or the neck and counting the pulse beats for 10 seconds. Then, multiply this number by 6. Even better, use a heart rate monitor.

If you don't have a stopwatch or clock to calculate an accurate heart rate, a good indicator that you are training in your desired aerobic zone is when you can't easily carry on a conversation but you are not yet out of breath.

Get ready to run.

should train the same way. In other words, you'll benefit more from training sessions that mimic a game than from just jogging or running for 30 minutes straight.

One well-known training method is *Fartlek* (Swedish for "speed play") conditioning, where athletes are literally put through their paces for a predetermined time. During Fartlek sessions, athletes work continuously but vary the intensity level to challenge the muscles and increase endurance.

Sample Fartlek session:

- Warm-up with a steady jog (10 minutes)
- Run hard at 75 percent of fastest-possible pace (90 seconds)
- Jog (45 seconds)
- Sprint (10 seconds)
- Run backward (30 seconds)
- Walk (30 seconds)
- Run hard (60 seconds)
- Repeat entire session three to four times

Note: Athletes should work at 60 to 80 percent of their maximum heart rate. Total session should last 45 minutes or longer.

CROSS-TRAINING

Although there is no better way to become a better rugby player than to play rugby, many coaches encourage players to vary their workouts occasionally in order to train muscles differently, which may improve performance. Cross-training, which can be as simple as participating in another activity once a week (such as biking, swimming, or working out on an elliptical trainer), may also help reduce the risk of injury from repetitive movements. Another benefit: cross-training may prevent boredom and possible burn-out.

Athletes may also want to cross-train in the gym by experimenting with resistance training apart from traditional weight-lifting. Here are some other workouts to try:

- **Pilates:** A series of very controlled, concentrated exercises performed to strengthen the core, great for rugby players who need to improve their balance.
- **Plyometrics:** A type of exercise (mostly involving squats and jumps) designed to produce fast, powerful movements. Want to explode on the field? Plyometrics may be for you.
- **Kettlebell lifting:** A type of exercise where athletes lift cast-iron weights (picture a cannonball with a handle) using total-body movements.

STRENGTH TRAINING

Why do ruggers hit the gym? Lots of reasons. When players work out with proper form, weight training can provide many benefits, including increased strength, speed, and confidence; improved flexibility and range of motion; greater "explosiveness" (which improves power movements such as jumping); and resistance to injury.

Although the topic is still controversial, especially regarding young players, the trend is definitely shifting toward incorporating some weight training along with other strength and conditioning exercises into rugby players' routines. Most trainers concur that even players as young as ten years old may benefit from doing calisthenics or using their own body weight (in exercises such as pull-ups, push-ups, skips,

---

According to Coach Tom Billups, rugby players should give special attention to the "upper triangle," the area extending from the little bump on the back of your skull to the middle of each shoulder blade, when training in the gym. Focus on pull-ups and Olympic style lifts to strengthen and stabilize the neck and shoulders, which are so crucial to tackling and binding. This is an excellent way to improve performance and prevent injury.

---

and jumps) to increase their strength. But as a rule, only players who have already gone through puberty (usually age fourteen) should start a regular weight training program.

WHAT TO WORK AND WHEN

Most athletes use the off-season to build up strength and power through weight training. During the season, they aim to maintain their off-season gains.

Some teams provide players with specific training plans and goals. Whether or not you have a written plan, it's a good idea to consult with your coach or a trainer about your specific routine.

In general, to develop maximum strength, an athlete should plan on four days of weight training a week (two days focusing on the upper body and two days working the lower body). These workouts are often combined with cardio by lifting weights first, then going for a run or a swim (always after a solid warm-up). Many athletes today also practice circuit training, a highly time-efficient gym workout in which they combine an aerobic workout and weight work at the same time by moving quickly from machine to machine without resting.

Circuit training is especially valuable when endurance (very important in rugby) is being emphasized over strength.

There are many excellent resources to consult regarding exercising with weights. Many players and coaches consult the websites http://rugbyfitnesstraining.com and http://www.fitness4rugby.com. Other good sources include *Supertraining* by Mel Siff and *The Strength and Conditioning Journal*, a magazine published by the National Strength and Conditioning Association.

TIP FOR PLAYERS

According to *The Ultimate Guide to Weight Training for Rugby*, variation is one of the keys to a great workout program. Your body will eventually adapt to any routine it's on, so it is very important to change routines once your gains have stopped and your strength has peaked (approximately every four weeks).

TRAINING TIP

"For an outside back, being powerful is more important than being strong. Once you have a basic strength base, try to incorporate plyometrics and complex training into your weights and sprints session to improve your explosive power. This will not only help your speed off the mark and your ability to change direction, but it will also make you more powerful in contact situations, whether you are powering through a tackle, making a tackle, or hitting a ruck or maul."—*Nicki Drinkwater, Outside Center, England*

THE BASICS

Here are a few basic weight-training exercises you can do using just a few free weights and a bench. Remember, during the season, most athletes work with lighter weights, performing a higher number of reps to increase endurance. But to increase strength (during the off-season) you'll want to lift slightly heavier weights for fewer reps. Off-season: Pick a weight you can lift slowly up to eight or nine times. On-season: Pick a weight you can lift slowly ten to twelve times.

Bench Press (works the chest)

Lie on your back on a bench. Your feet should be flat on the floor. Grasp one dumbbell in each hand, bend your arms, and hold the dumbbells at shoulder level, as close to the shoulders as possible. Slowly lower the weights to just above your chest, then raise them straight up, extending your arms fully.

Do three sets, 8 to10 reps each.

Military Press (works the shoulders)

Sit on the end of the bench, or stand up straight. Pick up the weights, and bring them to shoulder level with your elbows down at your sides. Lift the weights directly over your head, hold, then lower and return to starting position.

Do three sets, 8 to 10 reps each.

Biceps Curl (works the biceps)

Sit on the end of the bench, or stand up straight. Hold the weights with an underhand grip, resting them gently on the tops of your thighs. Bend your elbows, and lift the weights slowly up to your chest. Then slowly lower them, keeping arms in line with your shoulders.

Do three sets, 8 to 10 reps each.

STAND AND DELIVER

Often the best "weights" to use during training, especially for young players or those new to strength training, is your own body weight. The key is to use proper form and do the exercise slowly.

The following moves can be performed on the floor or a mat. Athletes can also do these exercises outside on the field. Some exercises require a medicine ball or its larger, lighter cousin, the stability ball. (Both medicine balls and stability balls are effective pieces of equipment because they are more pliable and less stable than the hard ground. The body has to work against a ball, pushing it down to keep it stable, which increases the benefit of the exercise.)

Deep-Knee Squat

- Stand with your feet hip distance apart and knees loose, not locked. (See the sidebar "It's Universal" on page 167 for a further description of the ideal stance.)
- Extend your arms directly out in front of you for balance.
- Keeping your knees behind your toes, slowly lower into a squatting position until your thighs are parallel to the floor.
- Slowly return to a standing position.
- Do three sets, 8 to 10 reps each.

Lateral Jumps

- Stand on your left leg.
- Jump sideways to your right (approximately 6 to 8 inches [15 to 20 cm]), and land on your right leg on the mat.
- Keep your right knee soft to absorb the force, and use your ankle, knee, and core to stabilize.
- Jump back to your left leg and repeat.
- Do three sets of 8 to 10 reps each.

Single-Leg Medicine Ball Reach

- Stand on your slightly bent right leg.
- Hold a medicine ball in front of your chest.
- Without dropping your chest toward the floor, rotate your torso 90 degrees to the right. Keep your head level and eyes on the ball.
- Return to start position.
- Do one set of 8 to 10 reps on each side.

Players with access to a gym, or even a few hand weights or dumbbells at home, can add the following exercise several times a week.

Dumbbell Push Press

- Begin standing with your knees slightly flexed.
- Hold dumbbells at shoulder level.
- Drive dumbbells straight overhead by extending your hips, knees, and ankles simultaneously.
- Finish with your arms straight overhead and knees slightly bent.
- Do three sets of 8 to 10 reps.

It's Universal

Trainers around the world are well acquainted with a stance known as the "universal sports position."

Top-level athletes in every sport, from golf to surfing to football, strike a pose at a key point in their movement where they are semi-crouched on the balls of their feet, with hands in front and torso centered over the lower body. They are balanced, prepared to move in any direction—front, back, left, right.

This position, also known as "the athletic stance," is perfect for rugby players, who perform many explosive movements (cutting, dodging, faking) during a game. So, if you want to boost acceleration, agility, and your vertical leap, start by getting your torso in line.

To begin, a player stands with his feet hip distance apart, toes and heels in line, knees slightly bent, and arms down at his sides. Next he brings his arms out in front of him—elbows are bent, palms are flexed slightly.

Bring it on. This guy is ready.

According to *The RFU Handbook of Safe Rugby,* a 30 percent gain in strength may be achieved following an eight- to twenty-week resistance training program.

CORE SUPPORT

A strong and stable core, also known as the midsection of the body where the abdominals, obliques, and back extensors help brace the spine, is incredibly important to rugby players who need to be able to move in every direction. All movements—every kick, dodge, fake, sprint—start from this area.

The following exercises are best done inside on a mat. You'll need a stability ball or medicine ball for most of the moves.

Bird Dog

- Begin on all fours, with your knees directly under your hips, your hands directly under your shoulders, and your feet parallel.
- Without arching your back, straighten your right arm and left leg so they form a straight line with the body. Keep your head down.
- Hold the position for eight counts, then lower your arm and leg.
- Do three sets of 8 to 10 reps on each side.

Forward Roll

- Kneel with your forearms resting on stability ball.
- Raise your hips so that your body is in plank position, with only your feet touching the ground.
- Maintaining a straight line from shoulders to feet, use your forearms to roll the ball forward until it's past your shoulders.
- Roll the ball back and return to the starting position.
- Do three sets of 8 to 10 reps each.

Supine Bounce

- Lie on your back with your legs straight and the stability ball between your feet.
- Without allowing your back to arch, raise your legs so that the ball is 2 inches (5 cm) above the floor.
- Release the ball so it bounces off the floor, then catch it between your feet.
- Do three sets of 8 to 10 reps each.

Pepper Catch

- Sit on the floor with your knees bent and your feet just slightly off the floor.
- Have a partner toss a medicine ball to you.
- Catch the ball, then stabilize and throw the ball back without twisting your hips.
- Do three sets of 8 to10 reps each.

TIP FOR PLAYERS

When the season starts, it's important to maintain the gains you made in your off-season workouts. Playing the game will partly accomplish this goal. But don't neglect additional training.

Back Extension

- Lie on your stomach on a stability ball with your chest hanging over the edge of the ball.
- Place your hands behind your head, elbows out to the sides, and lift your chest off the ball.
- Hold, then return to the starting position.
- Do three sets of 8 to 10 reps each.

Hip Raise

- Lie on your back on the floor with your feet on a stability ball, knees bent at a 90-degree angle.
- Raise your hips so that only your shoulder blades touch the floor.
- Form a straight line from shoulders to knees; hold.
- Lower your body back to the floor.
- Do three sets of 8 to 10 reps each.

Notes on Stretching

According to the American College of Sports Medicine, stretching, if done regularly and carefully, can increase range of motion in the joints, nourish muscle tissue, improve coordination and posture, and contribute to improved athletic performance. That said, the current school of thought discourages stretching cold muscles. In other

Training Tip

"Just because you play in the front row, don't assume it's all about being big, strong, and heavy. Nowadays, to play at a high level, the focus has moved toward being tough and powerful. Weight sessions are probably still the biggest part of a training program, but try to incorporate plyometrics and power lifts that will help you to apply your strength at speed, like you need to on a pitch." —*Sharon Whitehead, loosehead prop, England*

words, you should never start a workout by stretching. Stretch only after a warm-up or, even better, after a full workout.

Although for years coaches and athletes believed stretching could prevent injury, there have been no conclusive studies published to prove this. However, most trainers find that stretching can help an athlete recover from an injury. In any case, stretching improves flexibility, which is always a plus.

For a more detailed explanation of stretching, including diagrams of sample stretches, two good sources are the *Personal Trainer's Manual*, from the American Council on Exercise, and *Stretching* by Bob Anderson (Shelter Publications).

STRETCHING TIPS

- Stretch only when your body is warmed up.
- Never bounce while stretching.
- Stretch until muscles feel tight, but stop before you feel pain.
- Hold stretches for 10 to 30 seconds.
- Don't hold your breath while stretching. Take deep, full breaths.
- Stretch as often as possible—every day if you can.

FEED ME

Food is fuel for athletes. A blindside flanker who doesn't consume enough calories soon finds herself running out of steam, whether she's in the gym or out on the playing field.

Quantity is important. But what and when a player eats is just as important as how much she eats.

Despite the current low-carb trend, it's important for athletes to remember that they rely on carbohydrates for performance, especially wholesome, complex carbohydrates such as those found in multigrain bread or oatmeal. Athletes need to maximize glycogen (carbohydrate) stores during training as well as when it really counts—during competition.

Protein is an important part of the diet, but athletes may find that too much protein hinders their performance, since the body digests proteins relatively slowly. Therefore, it's especially important to avoid too much protein right before a game.

Every player should make it a point to formulate her own diet plan and experiment to find out what approach works best. (Just don't experiment on game day!) Coaches are a great resource for nutrition tips, and there are many excellent books on the topic of nutrition for athletes who play endurance sports such as rugby. (Check out *The Sports Nutrition Guidebook*, Third Edition, 2008, by Nancy Clark.)

WATER ALL!

In addition to eating a well-balanced diet, the best thing a player can do to enhance his performance and keep from feeling fatigued is to drink water. Hydration is extremely important, especially on match day. An athlete should remember to drink water throughout the day

Don't forget to hydrate.

before a game or a practice and throughout the day leading up to the game. If he waits to hydrate while playing, it may be too late.

According to the National Athletic Trainers' Association (NATA), a player should drink at least 16 to 20 ounces (0.5 to 0.6 l) of fluids approximately two hours before working out. Many coaches tell their players to drink up to 100 ounces (3 l) of water or water mixed with sports drinks in the course of a day, especially during the hottest months of the year.

Note: Although water should be your main drink, sports drinks are fine to put in the mix, especially after a game or practice when you need to replace electrolytes.

PRE-MATCH MEALS

The main goal of a pre-game meal is to elevate glycogen levels by eating foods rich in carbohydrates. Be sure not to eat so much food that you feel uncomfortable and won't be able to play well.

Here are some sample meals.

High Carbohydrate Dinner or Lunch (three to four hours prior to game)

- Chicken breast, mashed potatoes, vegetables
- Rice (steamed or boiled)
- Soup (avoid heavy or creamed soup, also chili)
- Baked potato (light butter, low-fat or no-fat sour cream)
- Deli sandwich (lean meats, veggies, light mayo, little cheese)
- Thick-crust cheese or vegetable pizza
- Peanut butter sandwich

- Grilled or roasted chicken sandwich
- Pasta salad with low-fat dressing
- Salads
- Pasta and marinara sauce with bread

High Carbohydrate Breakfast (three hours prior to game)

- Fruit
- Waffles
- Pancakes (light butter and syrup)
- Cold or hot cereal
- Low-fat yogurt
- Toast, bagel, English muffin, bran muffin
- Pasta or pasta salad
- Fresh fruit (apples, bananas, grapes, oranges)
- No greasy foods or heavy meats (hash browns, breakfast steaks, ham, or sausage)

Light Snacks (one to two hours prior to game in moderate quantity)

- Bagel or English muffin
- Raisins, dried fruit
- Yogurt with cereal or fruit
- Pretzels, unsalted peanuts
- Whole-wheat toast or bread
- Crackers
- Fresh fruit (apples, bananas, grapes, oranges)
- Popcorn (no salt/butter)
- Granola or energy bar
- Cold or hot cereal

Note: After the game, players should consume carbohydrate-rich fluids and foods as soon as possible (at least within one to two hours after hard exercise) to replace the glycogen they burned during the game.

NUTRITION TIPS

- Small, frequent meals are best in order to avoid energy dips caused by low blood sugar.
- Each meal should consist of a lean protein (chicken, tuna, tofu), fibrous carbohydrate (lettuce, cauliflower, cucumber), and healthy fats (olive oil, nuts, fish).
- Avoid high-fat and high-sugar snacks and meals. These can slow you down faster than a tough defender.
- Try to get your vitamins from real food as opposed to supplements. Energy from protein, minerals, and fiber is best utilized by the body when it comes from actual calories.
- On workout days, be sure to consume plenty of water—at least half your body weight in ounces. Example: If you weigh 140 pounds (63.5 k), drink 70 ounces (2 l) of water.
- Carbo-load throughout the week before a game and for the first four hours afterward for optimum recovery.
- Don't overeat late the night before a match. Also, try to eat a light breakfast the morning before a game or practice.
- Remember, during a workout or match you are burning what you ate and stored twenty-four to forty-eight hours earlier.
- Experiment with diet and hydration during practice—not on game day!
- Avoid the drive-thru and other places serving fast (i.e., high-fat) foods.
- Avoid food and drinks containing caffeine, since they cause dehydration.
- Aim for 60 percent of calories from carbs, 15 percent from protein, and 25 percent from fat.

Coming to Terms

Active rest: An easy activity designed to keep a player warm.

Aerobic: A stage of a workout when all of the body's need for oxygen is met by what is being inhaled and what is already stored in the body. This state can continue for a long time.

Agility: The ability to move quickly from one position to another, for example, rising from the ground to your feet or effortlessly changing your direction of running.

Anaerobic: A stage of a workout when the body's need for oxygen is not met by what is being inhaled and what is already stored in the body. This state cannot continue for long because it causes a painful buildup of lactic acid in the muscles.

Body composition: The proportion of muscle, bone, fat, and other vital parts in the body.

According to England's Josh Lewsey: "I would say that rugby, at the international level especially, is one of the most intense physical games there is. It tests all different facets of fitness. I don't think people realize just how tiring contact is. Wrestling with huge men just saps your energy."

7: GAME DAY

From Pre-Game Rituals to Top-Notch Tactics

Athletes playing competitive sports are creatures of habit. As the season gets underway, they get into their groove, with routines and rituals they use to prepare for every match. This involves what they do in the days leading up to a game as well as the day and hour before kickoff. Of course, what really counts is how they play when the clock is running, but what team doesn't need an edge?

> "To play rugby union, you need three things: A good pass, a good tackle, and a good excuse."—ANONYMOUS

Advance Team

Motivation

When it comes to stirring up team spirit, some teams take a more vigorous approach than others. As fans of international rugby know, many New Zealand teams, such as the All Blacks, take the field with a fierce-looking pre-game dance called the haka. According to legend, the haka originated in the early 1800s when chief Te Rauparaha of the Ngati Toa tribe was being chased by his enemies. After hiding in a pit, he climbed out to find someone standing over him. Instead of being killed, as he feared, Te Rauparaha was instead greeted by a friendly local chief. Elated, he burst into the haka.

The dance and accompanying chant can be tremendously intimidating to the opposing team, especially if they've never seen it before. This was dramatically demonstrated in the 2008 movie *Forever Strong* when the Highland Rugby Club performed the ritual before the U.S. National High School Championships as the opposing team stood and watched in stunned silence.

Superstition

Not willing to depend entirely on mere training and practice, many rugby players admit to wearing lucky socks or even lucky underwear to give them the edge on match day. Some, whose teammates consider themselves not so lucky, even resort to not washing their uniforms

In big league play, there are an average of 150 tackles and 150 rucks per match.

during a winning streak. Lewis Moody of the Leicester Tigers and England's National Team says he goes to the movies the night before every match, though he counts this as more ritual than superstition. Several of his teammates, however, show their superstitious side by refusing to shave for the duration of big tournaments.

Drew Mitchell of the Qantas Wallabies admits to playing with a lucky coin tucked into his sock. His teammate Berrick Barnes wore the same pair of green-and-white swim trunks under his uniform for five years. (As far as we know, he did wash them.) Around the world, some players claim that being the last to run through the tunnel and out onto the field brings them luck. Others insist that when they sit in the third row on the bus or send a text message to Mom right before a game, things will go their way.

PREPARATION

Lucky socks aside, many players and coaches have proven methods for getting into match mode. The week before a game is primarily about maintenance; as a rule, this is not the time to introduce new skills or try to improve physically. Although it is common for a coach to run his team through problem areas early in the week, for the most part, players should focus on reinforcing what they already know and not overdoing it.

Often, when it comes to preparing for a match, what players don't do can be as important as what they do. According to Cal Rugby Coach Jack Clark, "When you play a game on Saturday, you need to take a team run on Thursday and back-off on Friday to get your legs back."

GET YOUR MATCH HEADS ON!

On game day, the philosophy of game week still holds true: What you don't do can be as important as what you do. Try not to focus on a negative outcome. In other words, don't let the voice in your head say, "Do not drop the ball today!" Instead, visualize yourself holding on to the ball. Successful players and coaches swear by this technique!

Another way many players get their game on, and calm pre-match jitters at the same time, is to establish their own pre-game routines. Something as simple as walking the field by yourself can help you prepare for game time.

TIP FOR COACHES

Every pre-match warm-up should involve some sort of contact so players are truly game-ready.

Match day!

SHOWTIME

The best thing a player can do to be effective during a match is to focus on her core skills during practice. Mastery of fundamental skills, especially at the youth level, wins more games than complicated plays.

Still, every team needs a basic game plan. Often this is simply a matter of knowing your opponent's strengths and weaknesses as well as your own. For example, if the opposing team consistently wins every one of their line-outs, you should forget about trying to beat them during the throw-in and focus on stopping the mauls that follow. If your team has an exceptionally strong runner or kicker, make sure to get that player the ball as often as possible.

Since certain situations occur in every match, and there's very little time to think when they do, the coach and team captain should plan ahead as to how the team will react. *What should our post-penalty plan be? What is our preferred restart method? Is our team stronger on kicks, scrums, or line-outs?* These are things you can map out and practice ahead of time. But during the game, it will be up to the players to react quickly and call the shots.

Got game?

PLAN OF ATTACK

The goal of every rugby team is to win the ball, keep the ball, and score. Every team accomplishes this a little differently; often the most successful clubs win by adapting on the run. But for those looking to outline their strategy ahead of time, here are some options.

Ten-Man Plan

This strategy puts the spotlight on the eight forwards, the scrumhalf, and the flyhalf, while the backs are put on the proverbial back burner. The objective is for the forwards to handle the ball in a tight pack (supported in emergency situations by the scrumhalf and flyhalf) while they push downfield directly through the defending forwards. Backs focus primarily on defense. This plan is best when your team is strong up front.

All-Out Plan

This strategy involves all players attacking from all parts of the field at all times. The focus is on running to advance the ball in nearly every situation.

This plan is best for teams with excellent backs and players (at all positions) who are great runners.

Always think one step ahead.

TIP FOR PLAYERS

Even if your game plan is loose, try to decide which player you plan to distribute to if you win the ball. (Who is nearby? Who keeps beating his defender?) You'll have more time to think about this during set pieces than on the run, so before a scrum or a line-out, take a few seconds to visualize your receiver.

Plan C

Most youth teams and newer clubs create their own plans, taking into consideration the talent and experience of their players. Feel free to cut and paste the parts of other plans that work for you.

PASS PERFECT

In rugby, players pass by throwing the ball backward or laterally to a teammate. But every situation calls for its own type of pass, depending on where you are and what's happening on the field.

- **Cut-out pass (or miss pass):** A pass that deliberately misses one or more players in order to reach the next player in the attacking line

- **Dive pass:** A pass made while diving toward the intended receiver

- **Dummy pass:** A fake pass meant to deceive the defense

- **Forward pass:** An illegal pass that travels forward when released

- **Gut pass:** A hand-off made to a nearby teammate when the ballcarrier is under pressure

- **Lob pass:** A high, looping pass aimed to sail over the heads of opposing players

- **Pop pass:** A soft, floated pass that flies slightly upward into the space in front of the receiver

- **Scissors pass:** A pass made to a teammate after he reverses direction and cuts back in order to confuse the defenders

- **Screen pass:** A move where the passer uses his body as a screen to shield the pass from a defender's view; very similar to a gut pass

- **Spin pass:** Similar to a spiral in football; mostly used by scrumhalfs, but may also be used by other players, for speed, length, and accuracy

- **Switch pass:** A pass that hides the ball from the opposing team and changes the direction of the attack

Be ready for mud on the pitch.

Note: On rainy days, players should keep the ball as often as possible to avoid turnovers due to slippery hands. When it's wet outside, pass less, maul more.

The Best Defense

On defense, the primary goal is to regain possession of the ball. To accomplish this, your side must first stop the attack. The most effective strategy to defend against an attack (this should sound familiar by now) is to keep it simple. As David Ellis, National French RU and Gloucester RU assistant coach and well-known defensive specialist, puts it, "Limit the time, space, and therefore, the options."

The way to take away an attacker's time and space is by applying pressure. In other words, cover the attacker closely and don't let up. Defenders also want to prevent attackers from running to the outside and breaking away, a defensive strategy that's known as applying width. Last, they want to apply depth, which means having extra players waiting to catch a ballcarrier who breaks away and runs downfield. Tacklers often use the touchline as an extra defender, since driving a ballcarrier out of bounds means the defending team will get to make the throw-in during the line-out.

Players on defense need to learn to quickly evaluate what's happening on the field and then, even more quickly, make decisions and react. Communication is paramount. Defenders must talk to each other on the field, alerting teammates about the movement of the ball—who's got possession, where the ball is headed, which attackers are open and need to be covered, and so on.

Most teams apply one of two defensive strategies:

Man to Man

Defenders match up with and cover attackers one-on-one.

This approach is best for applying pressure.

Marking your man one-on-one.

Assisting on the drift.

Drift

Defenders adjust their position on the field and "drift," playing an area of the field rather than marking one attacker.

This strategy works best for applying width and depth.

PENALTY ACTION

As much as rugby refs strive to keep the game moving, inevitably, a penalty is called and the offended team is awarded the ball. Usually, they have the choice to take a penalty kick or form a scrum. When this happens, the team captain needs to consider factors such as field position, time remaining, the score, and how his team is playing in order to choose the best post-penalty option.

Penalty Kick

Depending on the kicker's range, the difficulty of scoring, the game score, and the time remaining, the captain may elect to have his team "go for three" by attempting a kick at goal (penalty goal). The ball is marked at the place of infringement and a tee is tossed to the kicker from the sidelines. He has one minute from this point to complete the kick. Meanwhile, the opposing team must remain still with their hands by their sides until the ball is kicked. Once kicked, the ball is considered in play. The attacking team is free to move downfield, and the opposing team may oppose.

After a penalty, the nonoffending team may also "kick for touch." This move, in which the kicker boots the ball out of bounds, is a good option if the kick is out of range for a penalty goal or if the clock is ticking and the team is behind by more than 3 points. Kicking for touch allows a team to advance downfield and usually results in a line-out with the other team throwing the ball in.

Free kicks, awarded for more minor infractions, also give the nonoffending team possession, with the choice of kicking for touch or forming a scrum.

Note: The nonoffending team may also choose to take a quick tap, a kick made through the mark where the foul occurred immediately after a penalty is called. This is an effective play in that it tends to surprise the defense before they have a chance to regroup. On the down-

Scotland's John Leslie is credited with the fastest try in international match history: He scored just nine seconds into his team's match against Wales at Murrayfield in 1999.

side, the kicking team loses the opportunity to gain a lot of territory or kick a 3-point penalty goal.

Scrum

The nonoffending team may choose to form a scrum at the point of infringement. Often they will do this if they have not been playing well during line-outs or if they are close to the goal line and in position to score. Since the attacking side is the one putting in the ball, they have the edge and almost always win the ball. But it's not unheard of for defenders to come up with possession by exploiting any weaknesses in the scrum, especially by splitting apart opposing front-row players who are not bound tightly together.

ACT AND REACT

Every play in a rugby match is a piece of a constantly moving puzzle. It's difficult to determine ahead of time exactly what to do from one play to the next, because, with very few exceptions, everything and everyone is moving! Plus, sides switch from attack to defense mode very frequently throughout the match, and it happens at lightning speed, often too fast for players to stop and think.

Still, there are certain things players should be prepared to do in different scenarios.

When to Kick

Kicking on the rugby pitch is much more than the play of last resort. Kicking can be a great weapon on both attack and defense. For example, if your side is killing 'em during line-outs, the flyhalf will want to kick for touch (and force a line-out) when he is feeling defensive heat. Or, if the defense is coming at you hard and fast, booting a grubber kick over their heads into the hands of your waiting teammates may be the best way to beat them and continue your march downfield.

Don't be afraid to use your feet!

After the Ruck

After winning the ball at the ruck, a player from the team with possession should strive to pass immediately to the scrumhalf, who has the best chance of running downfield before the defense can reorganize. To confuse the defense, the attacking team may want to use a "pick and go" move where the ballcarrier basically lies down and places the ball behind him as several teammates step over him (to push the defenders away) while another teammate scoops up the ball.

Winning the ball at the ruck.

Protecting the Ball during the Maul

Mauls are usually formed following line-outs or in situations where the ballcarrier makes contact with a defender and turns toward supporting teammates so as a unit they may protect the ball from defenders. Once the maul is formed, if the opposition prevents a roll around the edge of the maul, move the ball to the back of the formation and try to release it to your scrumhalf while you are still moving forward.

During the Scrum

Positioning is important when forming a scrum. As a rule, the best attacking position for a scrum is in the middle of the field because the opposition is forced to split their backs since they don't know in which direction the ball will go. Remember, a scrum formed near an opponent's goal line can result in a pushover try!

Wheeling the scrum (when players purposely turn the scrum by pushing together) can be a tactic for securing a turnover for the team not throwing in, because when the scrum turns past 90 degrees, it must be reset, and the other team gets the throw-in. If your opponent keeps wheeling your scrum, the front rowers should step sideways (in sync) against the direction of the push.

Best place for a scrum: far from the opponent's goal line.

Even if you don't win the ball, your side should always strive to push the opposition backward during the scrum.

Scrum half sweep.

"I basically try to take it easy before a match and try not to get too worked up. I think it's key not to think too much. You can over analyze, and if you do tip over the edge, it can be hard to get back." —SCOTTISH WINGER SEAN LAMONT

After the Scrum

Following the scrum, the scrumhalf will run, pass, or kick the ball away. A pass, basically a sweep of the ball from the ground into the hands of a nearby teammate, is the most common way to return the ball to play. If your team needs to gain a lot of ground, try a kick. If there are no open receivers and you see open space, run for it.

During and after the Line-Out

Since strategy changes from line-out to line-out, teams should practice plays ahead of time, give them code names, and designate a player to call the play before the throw-in. For example, one play could feature a different jumper, with the team following up with a maul. Yelling out plays in code helps to confuse the defense while letting your side know what they will do following the line-out.

Remember, when your team consistently wins the ball at the line-out, you have more attacking options. Often, it's smart to begin with a driving maul, then transition to a rolling maul. After the defense scrambles to try to stop it, the ballcarrier can peel off into the midfield or down the blindside.

Note: Dozens of specific plays and strategies are available on http://www.betterrugbycoaching.com. You'll also find several excellent books at this site that break down specific plays, including *The Line-out and How to Win It*.

THE STRONG, SILENT TYPE

Often, the image of the coach is a larger-than-life personality who constantly hollers at his players from the sidelines. Every rugby coach needs to develop his own style, but some of the best in the game say that less is more.

In international play, coaches are not even allowed to stand on the sidelines during a match. U.S. Women's National Team coach Kathy Flores says that in this situation, she will occasionally relay a message to her team through the team doctor or a staff member who is permitted on the field to bring water to the players. But even during college or club play, where coaches are allowed on the sidelines, Flores mostly keeps quiet.

"I need to be quiet because the players need to make the decisions," she says. "Hopefully, I've done my job. I've gone over it in practice, and we've talked about it. Now, it's up to them."

8: HEY COACH!

How to Start a Team from Scratch

Back in the 1800s, when rugby was still trying to figure out if it was football, soccer, or utter mayhem, teams often played without coaches, leaving it up to the captain and other team leaders to teach the newer players and make strategic decisions. This isn't just ancient history; Scotland's National Team played without a coach until as recently as 1971.

Perhaps this coachless tendency speaks to the free-flowing, play-on nature of the game. For experienced players who grew up with the oval ball, it just might work. But in places where rugby is still developing, players need direction.

STARTING UP

Coaches may have to start from scratch.

Because rugby is new to some areas, especially to many parts of the United States, someone interested in becoming a coach may actually have to start up the team. If the sport isn't sanctioned by a school, you may be talking about building the team from the ground up. Often, the coaches who undertake this challenge are current or former players who grew up in areas where rugby is popular. These new coaches are ambassadors for the sport!

So if your town doesn't have an established team looking for a coach, what's the best way to start from scratch?

Groundwork

Step one: Recruit another coach, an assistant coach or two (local P.E. instructors make great candidates), and a few interested volunteers to help. Nobody can start and coach a team on her own.

Step two: To coach a team, you need a team. Ask around and talk to kids. Consider recruiting players who have the season off from other sports. (Football players who are tied up in the fall are good candidates for spring rugby.)

Step three: Research playing facilities: When are they available, and what will they cost? Also, investigate transportation options such as renting buses or carpooling in volunteers' vehicles. Can you get funding for any of these costs, or will the team foot the bill? If players are going to have to pay to play, they'll need to know this up front.

Step four: Recruit a sponsor to pay for uniforms and equipment, or solicit donations from dedicated volunteers.

Step five: Sign up for a USA Rugby coach's clinic or online course. Contact other coaches in your area (or older players still participating in club play) to get advice.

Step six: Immerse yourself in the *Laws of the Game*.

TEAM EFFORT

Once the team is formed, it's time to divide up the duties among the assistants. If you are lucky enough to have more than one, assign one coach to supervise forwards and one to work with the backs. Also, if possible, designate a team manager, whose duties may include reserving fields, notifying players about practices and games, arranging transportation, and taking care of equipment.

Two heads are better than one.

When it comes to coaching rugby, showing is often better than telling. Watch live practices run by more experienced coaches, and stock up on how-to DVDs that you and your players can view together. You may also want to seek out experienced players (young and old) to attend practice and demonstrate skills for younger players, or invite more experienced coaches to run clinics for your team.

Finally, be sure to take advantage of resources on the Internet, such as the weekly e-mail of coaching tips from http://www.betterrugbycoaching.com.

TIP FOR COACHES

Often, one of the biggest challenges for coaches of new rugby teams is finding other teams to play. Since new clubs have very few restrictions on their schedules or precedents to follow, it's okay to schedule games against older or more experienced players. In other words, don't be afraid to "play up." Many high-school clubs play against college clubs. The challenge just helps them improve as a team.

Make it official.

ARE YOU CERTIFIABLE?

USA Rugby certification is not required for coaches, but it is highly recommended. (Note: Local unions or territorial unions may have separate requirements, so check with them first.) Background checks are required for all youth, high-school, and college coaches.

The Coach Development Program offers certification (valid for three years), workshops (Introductory Rugby and Developing Rugby Skills), and other terrific resources. Step one is to access the Coaches' Portal, the coaches' portion of the USA Rugby website. Membership is $20 per year. (http://www.usarugby.org)

What Makes a Good Coach?

Once he gets his team up and running, every rugby coach becomes a combination motivator, cheerleader, tactician, diplomat, role model, friend, teacher, and fellow fan. Anyone who dedicates himself to this task needs to be committed to his players and truly have a love of the game. Jim Thompson, founder of the Positive Coaching Alliance, identifies three keys to succeeding as a coach of young players.

1. Be a "double goal" coach. "Teachable moments present themselves constantly in youth sports, but they are lost if a coach is saddled with a win-at-all-cost mentality. Youth coaches who are not focused on both winning and using sports to teach life lessons should not be coaching kids."

2. Increase players' love of the sport. "A great coach will inspire athletes to love the sport, to want to improve, and to want to come to practice."

3. Be an open communicator. "Include players in a conversation about the life of the team. Conversations are more effective than lectures. Ask for suggestions regarding the team's goals, strategies, and tactics, and include players in team decisions."

In search of teachable moments.

SECRETS OF SUCCESS

According to Jack Clark, the longtime rugby coach at the University of California at Berkeley (winners of twenty-four of the twenty-nine National Collegiate Championships played since 1980), a good rugby coach tackles his job in the same manner as any successful coach.

"You want to create a culture on your team that makes it fun, enjoyable, hard, and rewarding," he says. "You should have some teaching and team-building skills. Plus, you need an annual training plan where you look at the twelve months of the year and divide them into cycles that make sense. You take preseason, in-season and develop curriculums for each of those cycles. Then, you craft activities and training and explain what the aims were, create repetition, and give feedback."

When it comes to game time, a coach also needs to know how to get out of the way and let his players play. Unlike in football, where coaches are calling the plays, rugby players often take their game and run with it—literally.

"Rugby is a very fun game to play," says Coach Clark. "There is a kind of authorship on the field irrespective of game plans and coaching philosophies that makes it fun. It's analogous to a fast break in basketball. We know some rules that need to be performed but we don't know who is going to perform them. That's rugby. The players get to decide quite a bit."

Putting players in position starts with trial and error.

TIP FOR COACHES

Many coaches in the United States, even at the college level, are dealing with players who have never played rugby. For this reason, initially placing players in their positions can be tricky. Often, it's accomplished through trial and error. Since all players need to have the same core skills, a good starting point for differentiating them is: Big guy? You're a forward. Fast guy? You're a back.

WHY COACH?

Whether you're coaching a start-up club or hoping to launch a coaching career, think before you leap.

"Coaching is a privilege," says Coach Clark. "Working with young people as they try to reach new limits and helping them get from where they are to where they want to be is exciting stuff. It's sobering stuff, too. You don't want to do anything that damages anyone. You don't want to do anything that doesn't help them in life. It sounds corny, but athletics teaches you a lot about yourself. It's about setting goals, putting a plan in place every day to reach those goals. My favorite aspect of the whole thing is team. I'm convinced that all the great things in this world happen by groups of people pointing their noses in the same direction as a team."

THINK POSITIVE, PLAY HARD

Some longtime players and coaches have been heard to say, "The half-hearted are the first to get hurt." In other words, if you constantly worry about getting hurt, you may indeed get hurt. Best to learn the fundamentals (how to tackle, how to fall), then play hard and without hesitation. Otherwise, why are we here?

Coach's Scorecard

Sometimes a coach is too knee-deep in practices, planning, and worrying about the game to notice when things are going well. Here are some signs a team is on the right track:

- When the coach gives instructions, players hop to it
- The coach sets realistic goals that are usually attained
- The coach treats every player the same way, and always with respect
- The coach understands players as individuals and acknowledges their efforts
- The players freely offer the coach ideas and comments
- Team spirit and camaraderie permeates the pitch

Coaching is a privilege.

Rugby Moms and Dads

The parents of players are an essential part of any successful sports program. But when it comes to rugby, which may be new to a school or community, supportive parents are crucial.

Champion the Coach

Parents can be part of the solution.

Probably the most important thing a parent can do for his son or daughter (besides support and encourage the player) is to support the coach. During the practice or game, this means that rugby moms and dads need to learn to keep mum and let the coach do the coaching. Coaches and, ultimately, clubs and leagues have to determine their own guidelines for working with parents. So there is no confusion, some clubs actually outline the expectations for parents' behavior in writing.

COACH-PARENT PARTNERSHIP*

Research shows that when parents and teachers work together a child tends to do better in school. It's the same in youth sports. The following are some ways parents can contribute to a Coach/Parent Partnership that can help the athlete have the best possible experience.

1. **Recognize the Commitment the Coach Has Made:**

   For whatever reason, you have chosen not to help coach the team. The coach has made a commitment that involves many, many hours of preparation beyond the hours spent at practices and games. Recognize his commitment and the fact that he is not doing it because of the pay! Try to remember this whenever something goes awry during the season.

2. **Make Early, Positive Contact with the Coach:**

   As soon as you know who your child's coach is going to be, contact her to introduce yourself and let her know you want to help your child have the best experience she can have this season. To the extent that you can do so, ask if there is any way you can help. If you get to know the coach early and establish a positive relationship, it will be much easier to talk with her later if a problem arises.

3. **Fill the Coach's Emotional Tank:**

   Coaching is a difficult job and most coaches only hear from parents when they want to complain about something. When the coach is doing something you like, let him know about it. This will help fill the coach's emotional tank and help him do a better job. It will also make it easier to raise concerns later if you have shown support for the good things he is doing. And just about every coach does a lot of things well. Take the time to look for them.

4. **Don't Put the Player in the Middle:**

   Imagine a situation around the dinner table in which a child's parents complain in front of her about how poorly her math teacher is teaching fractions. How would this impact the student's motivation to work hard to learn fractions? How would it affect her love of mathematics? While this may seem farfetched, when we move away from school to youth sports, it is all too common for parents to share their disapproval of a coach with their children. This puts a young athlete in a bind. Divided loyalties do not make it easy for a child to do her best. Conversely, when parents support a coach, it is that much easier for the child to put her wholehearted effort into learning to play well. If you think your child's coach is not handling a situation well, do not tell that to the player. Rather, seek a meeting with the coach in which you can talk with her about it.

5. **Don't Give Instructions during a Game or Practice:**

   You are not one of the coaches, so do not give your child instructions about how to play. It can be very confusing for a child to hear someone other than the coach yelling out instructions during a game. If you have an idea for a tactic, go to the coach and offer it to him. Then let him decide whether he is going to use it or not. If he decides not to use it, let it be. Getting to decide those things is one of the privileges he has earned by making the commitment to coach.

6. **Fill Your Child's Emotional Tank:**
   Perhaps the most important thing you can do is to be there for your child. Competitive sports are stressful to players and the last thing they need is a critic at home. Be a cheerleader for your child. Focus on the positive things she is doing and leave the correcting of mistakes to the coach. Let your player know you support her without reservation regardless of how well she plays.

7. **Fill the Emotional Tanks of the Entire Team:**
   Cheer for all of the players on the team. Tell each of them when you see them doing something well.

8. **Encourage Other Parents to Honor the Game:**
   Don't show disrespect for the other team or the officials. But more than that, encourage other parents to honor the game. If a parent of a player on your team begins to berate the official, gently say, "Hey, that's not honoring the game. That's not the way we do things here."

* Courtesy of the Positive Coaching Alliance.

But parents can do a lot more for their player than simply resist the urge to holler from the sidelines. Rugby moms and dads can get involved. Offer to help the team by volunteering to

- Assist the coach
- Keep score
- Run the clock
- Line the fields
- Manage equipment
- Chaperone trips
- Organize car pools or phone trees
- Set up a team website
- Become a referee
- Raise funds
- Organize advertising, marketing, and publicity for the team
- Plan a team party

> **Many coaches teach rugby skills using the IDEA approach: *Introduce, Demonstrate, Explain* the skill, and *Attend* to players as they practice.**

- Organize a booster club and manage the club's activities
- Organize coach and player clinics
- Assist in making schedules
- Assist during registration
- Photograph players or videotape games
- Create a yearbook or program
- Take players to a college or Super League game
- Organize the team's medical kit (with medical waivers and emergency information for each player)

When a Parent Is the Coach

One of the most challenging situations for a parent (and the player) is when the parent is also his son's or daughter's coach. Every parent-coach should strive to treat his or her child the same as everyone else on the team. This takes patience, dedication, and a little creativity. One coach who found himself in charge of his sixteen-year-old son's team

Expect the best from all your players, and even more if they're your kids.

enlisted an assistant, another father with a child on the team, so they could each be "in charge" of the other's kid whenever possible. Another parent-coach cautions never to complain about games, referees, or other players in front of your child.

Equal treatment is a noble goal, but most parent-coaches say it's all right to expect more from your child in certain ways. Talk to your daughter before the season, and tell her she needs to be a leader on the team. Encourage her to help you with equipment set-up and other logistics.

It takes practice for a coach to walk the fine line between not favoring her own child and being overly critical of her performance on the field. With a little thought and planning, however, coaching your own child can be an incredibly memorable and rewarding experience.

HITTING THE FIELD

PRACTICE PLAN

In the early 1990s, researchers at Michigan State University's Youth Sports Institute polled a group of young players who had dropped out of sports and asked them what would make them want to play again. The number one response? "If practices were more fun."

Kids of every age want to be active, especially young ones, so the better organized a coach is with his practice plan, the less time players will spend standing around and the more fun they'll have at practice. Jim Thompson recommends that every practice consist of the following:

- An opening ritual to signify the transition to being with the team
- Team conversations in which the coach engages the players in team business rather than standing up to lecture

- Instruction in new skills and tactics

- Conditioning

- Scrimmaging

- Drills and activities that remind players that rugby is fun

- Discussion of a life lesson in which the coach relates what's been learned in practice to other parts of the players' lives

- A closing ritual that sends players off with a positive feeling

Keep practice moving.

TIP FOR COACHES

Take notes during a game on things that need to be addressed during the next practice. (Then be sure to address them!) Have an assistant or parent videotape the game so you and the players can review it later.

SAFETY FIRST

Rugby has a reputation as a dangerous sport, especially among those who are unfamiliar with the mechanics of the game. So a rugby coach has a tremendous responsibility to make safety the first priority on the pitch. Her first order of business should be to make sure that every player wears properly fitting shoes, mouth guards, and other pads and that no one on the team wears anything that might cause injury to someone else.

Talk to your players about safety. Then talk to them about safety again.

Since a player can get hurt just as easily during practice as he can during a game, the coach needs to enforce safety rules on practice days the same way a referee would on game day. Coaches should be sure to complete first aid and CPR training provided by a nationally recognized organization such as the American Red Cross or the National Safety Council. (Check with your school or league—this may be mandatory.) Also, every coach must keep a list of emergency numbers and a well-stocked first aid kit on hand.

The first aid kit should include the following items:

- Cell phone
- Plastic bags (for ice)
- Mirror
- Flashlight
- Disposable plastic gloves
- Scissors

- Triangular bandages
- Roll gauze
- Square gauze pads
- Cotton balls
- Band-aids (all sizes)
- Saline solution

- Tongue depressors
- Peroxide
- Antibacterial soap
- Hydrocortisone cream

- Insect sting kit
- Safety pins
- Thermometer

Just as important as a well-stocked first aid kit is a well-thought-out emergency plan. Coaches may ask for a volunteer committee of parents to help organize the team's emergency plan, which should include creating an emergency response card that contains phone numbers and medical information for each athlete and spelling out how the team will deal with minor and major injuries.

P-R-I-C-E

According to the American Sport Education Program, coaches should use the **PRICE** method to aid an injured player:

P — Protect the athlete and injured body part from further danger or trauma.

R — Rest the area to avoid further damage and foster healing.

I — Ice the area to reduce swelling and pain.

C — Compress the area by securing an ice bag in place with an elastic wrap.

E — Elevate the injury above heart level to keep the blood from pooling in the area.

9: Make It Official

How to Keep Score, Keep It Safe, and Keep the Match Moving

In the early days of rugby, officially, there were no officials. If a team was fouled, the captain would simply turn to the schoolmaster, who stood on the sidelines (not on the field), and say, "We'll take our advantage, sir," or "We'll take the penalty."

By the 1880s, referees became a fixture on the field of this ever-evolving game. Although the laws of the game have changed dramatically over the years, one thing has remained the same: What the referee says *goes*. Players, coaches, and spectators do not challenge the referee in rugby. He is the first and last word on the pitch.

Who Are These Guys?

In many leagues, especially those with youth teams or new clubs, there may be only one referee on the field. But at higher levels of play, there may be several match officials: the referee, the touch judges, the substitution official, and sometimes even the television match official (TMO).

The ref directs the game.

The Whistleblower

The referee, the guy with the whistle, is the judge and jury on the field. There is no court of appeal. Rulings are final, and although a team captain or coach may question a call, a player who argues with a ref will likely be sent off from the game. This is called "dissent," and it is one of the worst things you can do in rugby.

The ref makes his decisions known using the three communication tools at his disposal: whistle, voice, and body position. He may consult with the other match officials on a ruling (if he is lucky enough to have them), but he makes the final call on every play. Other referee duties include orchestrating the coin toss, keeping the official time, keeping score, sending players off (known as giving them a "red card") for serious infractions, and overseeing substitutions and replacements.

Note: Since rugby refs often work alone, they are responsible for being in the right place at the right time—at all times. This requires stamina. Rugby refs need to be in great shape or they can't do their job. This is why the best candidates for rugby officials are often active players themselves.

The Guys with the Flags

Touch judges work the side of the field and signal to the primary referee using flags. Although they assist the ref by alerting him to fouls he may not have seen and by signaling the completion of penalty and conversion kicks, their main job is to establish where a line-out is formed and which team throws in after the ball has gone into touch. To signal this, the touch judge stands where the line-out will be taken and raises his flag overhead while pointing in the direction of the throw-in team.

Note: Touch judges cover as much of the field as the primary referees, so fitness is important! Any official who can't literally keep up with the game will be out of a job.

Switch 'Em Up

It wasn't that long ago that, barring a serious injury, the players who started a match played the entire game. These days, more substitutions are allowed. The person who keeps track is the substitution official, who signals a switch by holding up two numbers: one for the outgoing player, the other for the incoming player. This official is also an understudy of sorts—if a touch judge has to be replaced, the substitution official is handed a flag and pressed into duty.

Step Right Up

So, you want to make it official? The first step is to contact USA Rugby to find out the name of the referee administrator in your state. This

Let's Go to the Video

During televised matches (usually at the pro level), there is often another official on hand: the television match official (TMO), also known as the video referee. This official watches the game on TV monitors and, when asked, will consult with the referee on calls.

person (or referee liaisons at USA Rugby) can outline the procedure for getting licensed and direct you to your local referee organization and training classes in your district. USA Rugby's website includes everything from detailed Q&A on game situations to a full fitness program for referees. Also included is a chart of Match Official Training Courses listing the descriptions, requirements, prerequisites, and costs of all courses by level.

Be sure to connect with other officials in your local league. They're a great resource for upcoming clinics and work opportunities. Also, check out http://www.irb.com for all the latest developments and rule changes at the international level.

Go for the Flow

Most rugby referees share a common goal: to keep the game moving. And rugby's rules lend themselves well to that.

"I think the referee has a great opportunity to allow the game to flow," says Alex Sharland, an experienced Florida match official. "Advantage is written into the *Laws*, so the referee can acknowledge that a foul occurred but allow the game to continue while the offended team has the opportunity to do something with the ball. Why would you stop white from scoring when red made a mistake?"

**Be ready to keep
the pace.**

MANAGEMENT 101

To further advance the "play on" principle, referees can actively manage the game to keep things flowing. "There's advantage, which is in the *Laws*," says Sharland. "Then there's management, which is not in the *Laws* but is part of the referee's toolbox."

Of course, a referee is required to call the match according to the *Laws*. But as he becomes more experienced, he will learn to guide players in the direction he wants them to go without excessive stops

TIP FOR REFEREES

New refs can learn a lot by watching rugby on TV, especially where to take position on the field during set pieces and when plays transition from one phase to another.

and starts. One way to accomplish this is to stop an offense before a player commits it. The ref who manages a game is like a traffic cop who warns a driver to slow down to prevent an accident, as opposed to the policeman who sets a speed trap hoping to write a ticket.

"You're directing in a way," Sharland explains. "Hey, red 3, leave him alone! So red 3 backs away. What he did or was about to do wasn't material to the game, so you don't stop the game." But if the player continues to transgress, or the play is in any way unsafe, even the best game manager will be forced to call a penalty. According to Sharland, "You have to know your law and know your game in order to know when you should and when you shouldn't call a foul."

Good refs also play the role of teacher or coach for young teams by giving warnings, direction, and instructions during matches. According to *Rugby for Dummies*, players can learn more during one match with a good referee than in a dozen practice situations.

Safety First

Perhaps the referee's most important function is ensuring the safety of the players. So, before the start of every match, referees should inspect the playing field. This is an important point for new clubs who may have access only to less-than-stellar facilities. Officials should look out for broken glass, rocks, sprinkler heads, and holes. Next, either the referee or the touch judge is required to inspect the players' clothing and boots. Anything found to be in violation of the *Laws*, along with anything the referee deems to be unsafe, must be removed at this point, no questions asked.

During the match, it's essential that referees and coaches work together to ensure the safety of all players. Referees should be certified

Former England halfback Adrian Stoop refereed the 1921 East Midlands versus Barbarians match. Somehow he managed to blow the final whistle 14 minutes early. After complaints and protests, the players and referee had to get out of their baths and return to the pitch to finish the match.

—RUGBY FOR DUMMIES

What the official says goes.

in CPR and first aid, and they must make sure to have a fully stocked medical kit and emergency plan for games and tournaments. Sources such as *The RFU Handbook of Safe Rugby* and the *Medical and Safety Guide* at http://www.usarugby.org offer useful tips on first aid, injury prevention, emergency action plan development, on-field injury treatment protocols, and procedures for resuming play after an injury has caused a halt.

STOPS AND STARTS

Unlike in football, where the clock counts down, in rugby, the clock counts up. In other words, the clock (set for a 40-minute half) begins running forward at the kickoff. As official timekeeper, the referee makes the call to stop the clock for injuries, for water breaks, to confer with team captains, coaches, or other officials, or when a player needs to replace a damaged or bloodied uniform.

To stop or not to stop? The referee's judgement is critical when it comes to stopping the game for injuries. If a player needs to be treated, most refs will stop the game and add some time to the clock to compensate for the stoppage. He also has the option of deciding not to stop the clock if the player is not seriously hurt and is not in other players' way. Of course, a serious injury always warrants a halt to the game so the player may be treated or removed from the field.

TIP FOR PLAYERS

Read the *Laws of the Game*. All of them. The whole way through. This may sound boring and cumbersome, but you'll gain a better understanding of what to do and what not to do on the field that could take years to learn through trial and error. It's best to download the most recent version from http://www.irb.com, since the *Laws* is constantly changing.

GET IN GEAR

Referee uniform:

- Referee shirt (colors vary by league; usually yellow, red, blue, green, or black)
- Shorts
- Badge or patch
- Cap
- Comfortable black turf shoes or cleats
- Knee socks
- Rain gear

Referee equipment:

- Gear bag
- Bag for wet shoes and clothes
- Flag set
- Cards (red and yellow)
- Whistle and lanyard
- Scorepad (waterproof or water resistant)
- Pen or marker
- Flip coin
- Countdown timer
- Watch
- First aid kit (see http://www.sportssafety.org for suggested contents)

CODE OF CONDUCT

According to *The RFU Handbook of Safe Rugby*, coaches and players should always

- *Accept the referee's decision*
- *Play fair*
- *Treat opponents with respect*
- *Win modestly and lose with dignity*
- *Thank the referee and opponents for the game*

In 1885, referees began using whistles. Soon after, in 1893, refs became fully responsibility for all aspects of the game.

REFEREE SIGNALS

As in almost every sport, the referee uses signals to call fouls and communicate other on-field developments to players, coaches, and spectators. In rugby, the signals tend to mimic the action—think of charades for referees. Here are the standard signals every rugby ref needs to know:

1. Penalty kick

3. Try and penalty try

5. Scrum awarded

2. Free kick

4. Advantage

6. Forming a scrum

7. Throw forward/ forward pass

8. Knock-on (move hand back and forth)

9. Not immediately releasing ball in the tackle

10. Tackler not releasing tackled player (open and close arms)

11. Tackler or tackled player not rolling away (make a rolling motion away from the body with the finger and arm)

12. Entering tackle from wrong direction (sweep arm in a horizontal semicircle)

13. Intentionally falling on a player (move arm in direction player fell)

14. Diving to ground near tackle (extend straight arm forward)

15. Unplayable ball in ruck or tackle (point arm to team that will throw in, then point arm and hand toward the other team's goal line while moving it back and forth)

16. Unplayable ball in maul (swing hand across the body to opposite shoulder)

During the first-ever international match in 1871, things got heated between England and Scotland after a contested try, which was finally awarded after a lengthy argument. Scottish umpire Dr. H. H. Almond then said, "When an umpire is in doubt, I think he is justified in deciding against the side which makes the most noise. They are probably in the wrong."

17. Joining a ruck or a maul in front of the back foot or from the side

18. Intentionally collapsing ruck or maul

19. Prop pulling down opponent

20. Prop pulling opponent on (gripping the chest, arm, sleeve, or collar)

21. Wheeling scrum more than 90 degrees (rotate index finger above head)

22. Foot up by front-row player

23. Throw-in at scrum not straight (imitate action of diagonal throw-in)

24. Failure to bind fully (stretch out one arm, move opposite hand up and down arm)

25. Handling ball in ruck or scrum (make sweeping motion)

26. Throw-in at line-out not straight

27. Closing gaps in line-out (draw hands together)

28. Barging in line-out

29. Leaning on player in line-out (move arm downward)

30. Pushing opponent in line-out (make pushing gesture)

31. Early lifting and lifting in line-out (make lifting gesture)

32. Offside at line-out (move hand and arm horizontally across chest)

33. Obstructing in general play

"Without the referee, thirty players can't have a game. But remember, it's not the ref's game, it's the players' game."—REFEREE ALEX SHARLAND

The number of certified referees in the United States has nearly doubled since 2005. The number of female referees has increased from 91 in 2005 to 181 at the end of 2007, while the number of male referees climbed from 716 in 2005 to 1,338 in 2007.

34. Offside at scrum, ruck, or maul (extend arm straight down and move from side to side)

35. Offside choice: penalty kick or scrum

36. Offside under 10-meter law or member of offending team failed to retreat 10 meters (10.9 yd) from point of infraction during penalty or free kick

37. High tackle/foul play

38. Stamping/foul play: illegal use of boot (make stamping motion)

39. Punching/foul play (clench fist and punch into open palm)

40. Dissent: disputing referee's decision (open and close hand to imitate talking)

41. Award of drop-out on 22-meter line

42. Ball held up in in-goal

43. Physiotherapist needed

45. Bleeding wound

44. Doctor needed

46. Timekeeper to stop and start watch

Red-Carded Ref: At a Plymouth club game in England in 1967, the referee sent off the touch judge after he participated in a melee with players and fans.

CRYING FOUL

In rugby, the punishment is meant to fit the crime. The worse the infringement, the more severe the penalty. The foul play law divides offenses into four levels: obstruction, unfair play, repeated infringements, and misconduct.

Obstruction basically covers simple penalties, often those committed unintentionally during play. *Unfair play* covers more intentional actions, such as a player's throwing the ball into touch to slow a game down. *Repeated infringements* are infractions a player commits after having been warned, so they are punished more severely, often with a yellow card. Lastly, misconduct—the most serious—means dangerous offenses such as tackling a player above the shoulders. These are punished by a yellow or red card.

SIN BIN

When a player is shown a yellow card, he is sent to the "sin bin" (penalty box) for 10 minutes. This not only serves to sternly warn the player for his actions (which will result in him being sent off if he repeats the infringement) but penalizes his team, which is forced to play with only fourteen players while he sits out.

COMING TO TERMS

Advantage: When the nonoffending team, following an infringement, takes the opportunity to develop play, gains some of their opponent's territory (tactical advantage), and perhaps even scores.

Drop out: A drop kick awarded to the defending team after the ball is made dead by the defense in the in-goal area. The kick may be taken anywhere along or behind the 22-meter line.

Fair catch (mark): Cleanly catching the ball directly from an opponent's kick (excluding the kickoff) inside the 22-meter line or the in-goal area. (Player calls, "Mark!" to indicate that she is making a fair catch.)

Foul play: Any infringement of the written rules or intended spirit of the game, including obstruction, unfair play, misconduct, dangerous play, unsporting behavior, retaliation, and repeat offenses.

Free kick: A kick awarded for a fair catch, or to the nonoffending team in the case of a penalty, per the *Laws of the Game*. A goal may not be scored from a free kick.

Infringement: Breaking one of the laws of the game.

Mark: The point where a free kick or penalty is awarded. Also refers to a player who catches a kick inside his own 22-meter line while calling "Mark!" Also refers to the act of guarding, staying close to, or covering another player.

Obstruction: When a player unfairly gets in the way of an opposing player.

Offside: During regular play, a player is offside (and temporarily out of the game) if he is either in front of a teammate carrying the ball or in front of the player who last played the ball. Onside: A player is onside (and may participate fully in the match) during loose play if he is behind a teammate with possession of the ball or behind the player who just played the ball or if he is behind the imaginary offside line during rucks, mauls, scrums, and line-outs.

Penalty kick: A kick (taken at goal) awarded to the nonoffending team after an infraction by their opponents.

Red card: The card shown to a player when the referee is sending him off for the remainder of the game.

Yellow card: The card shown to a player by the referee when he has committed foul play, a professional foul, or a repeated infringement. Punished by 10 minutes in the penalty box.

Resources

Kudu Rugby
(866) 583-8784
http://www.kudurugby.com

Rugby America, Ltd.
1215 E. Clary St.
Petersburg, IL 62675
(217) 632-0119
http://www.liquidrugby.com

Scrummaster
900 Whittaker Rd.
Box 71, MALAHAT BC
Canada, V0R2L0
(866) 990-9444
http://www.scrummaster.com

Tru Mark Athletic Field Marker
P.O. Box 706
Norfolk, NE 68702-0706
(800) 553-MARK (6275)
http://www.athleticfieldmarker.
   com

**Under Armour Performance
   Apparel**
1010 Swan Creek Drive
Baltimore, MD 21226
(888) 7ARMOUR (888-727-
   6687)
http://www.underarmour.com

**World Rugby Shop
A Division of 365 Incorporated**
3027 6th Avenue South
Birmingham, AL 35233
(800) 874-1001
http://www.worldrugbyshop.com
http://www.flagrugby.com

PERIODICALS AND WEB SITES

Rugby Magazine
(845) 359-4225
http://www.erugbynews.com
http://www.americanrugbynews.
   com
http://www.de-fence.co.uk
http://www.planet.rugby.com
http://www.redcross.org
http://www.rugby365.com
http://www.rugby-coach.com
http://www.rugby.com.au
http://www.rugbydirt.com
http://www.rugbyheaven.com
http://www.rugbyrugby.com
http://www.ruggers.com
http://www.sportssafety.org
http://www.usacollegerugby.com
http://www.zonewarrior.com

BIBLIOGRAPHY

Anderson, Bob. *Stretching: 20th Anniversary Revised Edition*. Bolinas, CA: Shelter Publications, 2000.

Biscombe, Tony and Peter Drewett. *Rugby: Steps to Success*. Champaign, IL: Human Kinetics, 1998.

Brown, Mathew, Patrick Guthrie, and Greg Growden. *Rugby for Dummies*. Hoboken, NJ: John Wiley & Sons, 2007.

Clark, Nancy. *Sports Nutrition Guidebook*. Champaign, IL: Human Kinetics, 2008.

Greenwood, Jim. *Total Rugby*. 4th ed. London: A&C Black, 1997.

Murray, Bill. *The World's Game: A History of Soccer*. Champaign, IL: University of Illinois Press, 1996.

Price, Robert G. *The Ultimate Guide to Weight Training for Rugby*. 2nd ed. Chicago, IL: Price World Enterprises, 2007.

Richards, Huw. *A Game for Hooligans: The History of Rugby Union*. Edinburgh: Mainstream Publishing, 2007.

Robinson, Derek. *Rugby: A Player's Guide to the Laws*. 4th ed. London: Collins Willow, 2002.

Rugby Football Union. *The RFU Handbook of Safe Rugby*. London: A&C Black, 1998.

Scally, John. *Odd Shaped Balls: Mischief Makers, Miscreants and Mad-Hatters of Rugby*. Edinburgh: Mainstream Publishing, 2005.

Siff, Mel. *Supertraining*. 6th ed. Denver, CO: Supertraining Institute, 2003.

Thompson, Jim. *Positive Sports Parenting: How Second-Goal Parents Build Winners in Life Through Sports*. Portola Valley, CA: Balance Sports Publishers, 2008.

————. *The Double-Goal Coach: Positive Coaching Tools for Honoring the Game and Developing Winners in Sports and Life*. New York: HarperCollins, 2003.

————. *Positive Coaching: Building Character and Self-Esteem through Sports*. Palo Alto, CA: Warde Publishers, 1995.

Williams, Tony and Frank Bunce. *Rugby Skills, Tactics and Rules*. Richmond Hill, Ontario, Canada: Firefly Books, 2008.

INDEX